FREEING THE HEART AND MIND

His Holiness the Forty-First Sakya Trizin

Freeing the Heart and Mind

Part 1: Introduction to the Buddhist Path

His Holiness Sakya Trizin

Edited by Khenpo Kalsang Gyaltsen
and Ani Kunga Chodron

WISDOM PUBLICATIONS • BOSTON

Wisdom Publications
199 Elm Street
Somerville MA 02144 USA
www.wisdompubs.org

Library of Congress Cataloging-in-Publication Data
Nag-dban-kun-dga'-theg-chen-dpal-'bar, Sa-skya Khri-'dzin, 1945–
Freeing the heart and mind. Part 1, Introduction to the Buddhist path / His Holiness
Sakya Trizin ; edited by Khenpo Kalsang Gyaltsen and Ani Kunga Chodron.
p. cm.
ISBN 0-86171-638-8 (pbk. : alk. paper)
1. Sa-skya-pa (Sect)—Doctrines. 2. Buddhist meditations.
I. Kalsang Gyaltsen, Khenpo. II. Peak, Lois. III. Title.
BQ7672.4.N345 2011
294.3'4432—dc22
2011007535

ISBN: 978-0-86171-638-8
eBook ISBN: 978-086171-614-2

15 14 13 12 11
5 4 3 2 1

Cover Photo: Toni Cervantes Copyright 2011,
www.tonicervantesphotography.com

Cover design by JETL. Interior design by Gopa&Ted2.
Set in Galliard 10.5/16.

Wisdom Publications' books are printed on acid-free paper and meet the
guidelines for permanence and durability of the Production Guidelines
for Book Longevity of the Council on Library Resources.

Printed in the United States of America.

This book was produced with environmental mindfulness. We have elected to print this
title on 30% PCW recycled paper. As a result, we have saved the following resources:
20 trees, 6 million BTUs of energy, 1,885 lbs. of greenhouse gases, 9,079 gallons of water, and
551 lbs. of solid waste. For more information, please visit our website, www.wisdompubs.org.
This paper is also FSC certified. For more information, please visit www.fscus.org.

Contents

Preface

EVERY STRUCTURE needs a strong foundation. So, too, study and practice of the precious Dharma needs a strong foundation in order to progress through the various stages and levels. Without a strong foundation, it is very difficult to understand and achieve the levels of the Dharma. The Vajrayana—or tantric—path has foundations that it shares with all Buddhist paths, and it has foundations that are unique to Vajrayana. Of these, it is most essential to master the shared foundations.

The mind is like an untamed horse galloping aimlessly in the wilderness of cyclic existence. Contemplation is the saddle to train the mind, and the holy Dharma is the rein to guide it upon the path to enlightenment. Therefore, it is of utmost importance to study and reflect upon the foundational teachings of Lord Shakyamuni Buddha and the commentaries on those teachings that were taught by great accomplished masters in ancient times.

At the same time it is also essential to learn the life stories of these great masters and to absorb the valuable principles within them into our daily lives. This will help us to turn our minds toward the Dharma and to set out steadfastly on the Dharma path, thereby enabling us to help other mother sentient beings achieve peace, happiness, and liberation.

I am very pleased to offer this first book of a Buddhist curriculum prepared for English-speaking students who wish to study the authentic

Dharma from the great masters of Tibet just as it has been taught for centuries by the Sakya order's greatest teachers. Although students may live at a distance in time or space from these great masters, careful study of this book will provide them with a strong foundation.

The Dharma teachings chosen for this curriculum are authentic and very traditional, yet they are offered in a modern format, with a study guide available at www.hhthesakyatrizin.org. After thoroughly studying these great teachings, you may wish to take the online examination on the website to measure your progress.

Learning about the Dharma proceeds through the stages of study, contemplation, and then meditation. After learning these teachings and thinking carefully about them, it is important to practice the meditations described here again and again. I believe this book will prove very beneficial for those who wish to learn about Buddhadharma in depth on their own, in their leisure time.

I thank Khenpo Kalsang Gyaltsen and Ani Kunga Chodron for editing this book and compiling the study guides, and Reverend Jamyang Tharchin for additional assistance. I wish this project every success and pray that these teachings will help to open the minds of those who seek the Dharma.

May the blessings of the Triple Gem be with you now and always.

His Holiness the Forty-First Sakya Trizin

PART ONE
Entering the Dharma Path

His Holiness Sakya Trizin

The first section of this book is a teaching I gave to a young friend who requested from me an introduction to Buddhism. In order to set him properly on the path, I explained the basics of Buddhist teachings with a special focus on the Buddha's most famous teaching, the four noble truths.

Introduction to Buddhism

His Holiness Sakya Trizin

WHATEVER PRACTICE WE DO, the direction in which it will lead us
depends on our primary motivation. Since having an improper motivation is very harmful, cultivating a suitable motivation—the highest motivation—is of utmost importance. The highest motivation for
receiving teachings is to attain full enlightenment not just for the sake
of ourselves but for the sake of all sentient beings. Thus, think that
you are receiving these teachings in order to accomplish this altru-
istic aim.

The basic progression of practice in the schools of Buddhism—
the Theravada, Mahayana, and Vajrayana schools—is to first establish a basis of sound moral conduct, then to study, contemplate, and
meditate. All Buddhist schools begin with the establishment of sound
moral conduct. Therefore, the very first thing is to receive the teachings with the right motivation and the right conduct. This means we
receive them with a physical, verbal, and mental attitude of respect.
Receiving teachings in this way is of great benefit.

According to Buddhist sutras, every sentient being, not only human
beings but every sentient being, from tiny insects up to even the highest gods, possesses buddha nature. Buddha nature is the true nature
of our minds. It is pure. It is never stained by obscurations. Therefore,
every living being, when it meets with the right causes, right conditions, and right methods, has the potential to attain perfect enlightenment, buddhahood.

But at the moment we do not see the true nature of our minds. Instead, our minds are completely deluded by two types of obscurations: obscurations that are defilements and obscurations of knowledge. As long as we have these obscurations, we are not free. Our path to buddhahood is blocked, and we are instead mired in what is known as *samsara*. *Samsara* is our deluded universe, the cycle of existence that goes on and on.

We have both a physical body and a mind. Of course we know where the physical body came from, how it developed, and how it is maintained. We can see it with our eyes, touch it with our hands, and can describe its size, color, shape, and so on. Eventually, when we leave this world, the physical body will be cremated, buried, or something else. But the mind is something very different. The mind is something that we can't see with our eyes; we can't touch with our hands; we can't describe in terms of shape, color, or size. Where does this mind come from? It cannot come from the body, which is something visible, because the mind is invisible. An invisible mind cannot rise from a visible physical entity—from matter or from the elements.

The mind also has to have some kind of continuity. It cannot come from nothing. Because of this we can establish or prove that we had a mind before we took our present physical body. We must have had a previous or past life. And before that life, we had another past life and so on. There is no point in time that we can identify as the beginning of a particular person's mind. Our minds are beginningless.

It is one of the wonders of life that from beginningless time until now, this same mind has continued. Of course it changes from moment to moment, but it is still in some sense the same mind. Never stopping, it continues even today in our present human form, but when we leave this world, it will enter another body in another world, in another place, in another family. This goes on and on. Therefore, our universe, or samsara, is like a circle or a wheel that turns and turns without end. Because samsara is like a wheel, it is called the *wheel of life*, and every segment of the wheel of life is characterized by some form of suffering. The Buddha taught the way to escape the wheel of life.

THE FOUR NOBLE TRUTHS

The very first teaching that the Buddha gave is known as the four noble truths. These four are the noble truths of suffering, of the cause of suffering, of cessation, and of the path to cessation.

The Noble Truth of Suffering

As long as we have obscurations and defilements, we will continue to be caught up in samsara. As long as we are in samsara, we will not be free from suffering. Generally speaking, no one is free from the four major sufferings: the suffering of birth, the suffering of sickness, the suffering of aging, and the suffering of death. In addition, among human beings, the wealthy have mental sufferings and those without wealth have physical sufferings, such as hunger, thirst, and exposure to the elements. As we read in the news, unhappy situations occur every day. Samsara is full of suffering.

According to Buddhist teachings, the universe of samsara is divided into six realms: three lower realms and three higher reams. The three lower realms are the hell realm, the hungry ghost realm, and the animal realm. The amount of suffering in the hell realm is unimaginable. The hungry ghost realm also has great suffering from extreme hunger and thirst. We can see for ourselves how much animals suffer. These are the three lower realms.

The three higher realms are the human, demigod, and god realms. A demigod is midway between a god and a human being. Demigods suffer greatly because, by nature, they are very jealous and are always competing with the gods. Yet because their merit is never equal to that of the gods, they are always defeated and suffer greatly. According to the Buddha's teachings, gods inhabit many different heaven-like realms. The gods have a very luxurious and high state. They have great enjoyment, a very long life, beautiful bodies, and so on; but they are also impermanent. One day, their beautiful life ends, and again they descend to the less pleasurable existences.

According to the Buddha's teachings, from the highest heaven to the lowest hell, all of samsara is nothing but suffering. Even what we see as enjoyments are actually a source of suffering. To see why this is so, we must understand what the teachings call the three kinds of suffering: the suffering of suffering, the suffering of change, and the suffering of conditional nature.

The *suffering of suffering* refers to what we normally consider to be suffering—physical pain, mental anxiety, misfortune, and so on.

The *suffering of change* refers to feelings that we normally consider as pleasurable, but that are, in reality, another kind of suffering. For example, a person who moves from very poor accommodations into a house with all the modern comforts and luxuries will feel very comfortable and happy by comparison. If that comfortable new house were the cause of happiness, the longer he stayed in it, then the happier he should become. But that is not the case. Even with every luxury and comfort, were he to stay in that place for a very long time, he would again feel bored and wish to do something else. This is why feelings we consider to be pleasure are in reality another kind of suffering, the suffering of change.

Finally, due to the *suffering of the conditional nature* of all phenomena or of all things, even what we normally consider to be feelings of indifference are also a kind of suffering. Not only moments of pain or of pleasure, but every moment of our lives in samsara is infected by an uneasiness and dissatisfaction that comes from misapprehending the way things are. This means that as long as we are in this cycle of existence, there is nothing but suffering. Wherever we go, with whomever we associate, whatever we do, we are never satisfied, and there is always something to complain about. The entirety of samsara, the whole cycle of existence, is nothing but suffering. This is crucial to realize.

The Buddha said that we must realize and know that life is suffering. Of course we suffer whether we recognize this or not. But when we don't have obvious sufferings, we tend to forget. The reason it is important to know that life is suffering is because until we know about suffering, we will not apply the remedies necessary to overcome that suffering. It is like when we are sick with a disease. First we need to diagnose the sickness correctly, for if we don't know the true nature of the sickness, the treatment we apply will likely be the wrong one.

To realize the first noble truth is to realize that life is suffering, samsara is suffering; all of samsara, from the highest heavenly realm to the lowest hell, is nothing but suffering. Once we know this, we produce what is known as *renunciation*, the wish to completely eradicate suffering. That is why we contemplate the descriptions of the sufferings of samsara, to develop renunciation. For it is this genuine feeling of renunciation that compels us to apply the necessary remedies.

The Noble Truth of the Cause

The second truth is the truth of cause: what causes the suffering, who causes the suffering, the reason we suffer.

There are many different religions. Some religions believe in a God, in the sense of a creator who created everything. God created life. God gives you happiness. God also punishes you and makes you suffer. According to Buddhists, however, there is no such God as this, no creator who judges and punishes.

According to the Buddha's teachings, all of life, everything that we experience now, is a product or projection of our own past actions, or *karma*. We perform actions all day long—physical, verbal, and mental actions—and every time we do an action, it is like planting a seed on fertile ground; it will produce a result. The good things that we experience and the bad things that we experience are not the product of outside forces. The good things and bad things that we experience are the product of our own actions. This is the second truth, the truth of the cause—the cause of suffering.

Why do we create the causes of our own suffering? Basically the reason we cause ourselves so much suffering is due to ignorance, to not knowing reality and not seeing the true nature of mind. Instead of seeing the true nature of the mind, our buddha nature, we cling to the notion of a self. And it is this clinging or attachment to a self that in turn brings about all our faults and thereby all our sufferings. We do this without any logical basis, for in reality there is no self.

The self is a mistaken notion, for if there were actually a self, it would have to be our name, our body, or our mind. Name of course is empty of the self. Any name could be given at any time to anybody. So the name is empty of self. As for the body, if we investigate every part of the body from the head to the toe, there are many different parts—flesh, blood, bones, and so on—but there is no single thing that can be called the self. The mind is something that is invisible. It is changing every moment. For example, the mind we had as small children and the mind we have as adults are very different. The mind changes, not just once in a while, but constantly, in every moment. Something that is always changing cannot be the self that we cling to. We mistakenly believe in a permanent self that is stable and unchanging.

In common usage, when we say "my house," we refer to a house that belongs to *me*. Similarly, we say "my body," which means the body that belongs to *me*. So when we say "my mind," it means the mind that belongs to *me*. Now, who is this me that owns all these things? Who owns our house, our possessions, our body, our mind? This big owner is the self. But where is that self? When we try to find where the self is located and who it is, nothing can be found anywhere.

It has been our habit from beginningless time to cling to the notion of a self. Our tendency to cling to a self is very strong and feels utterly natural to us, but it is this clinging to a mistaken notion of self, with no logical basis, that is the root of all faults. This is because when we cling to the idea of a "self," there naturally arises the idea of "other," like right and left. If there is a right side, there must be a left side. When we cling to self, therefore, then naturally there is attachment to our own side and anger toward others.

To put it another way, there are three root defilements: desire, anger, and ignorance. Ignorance is the most basic of these. The very root of ignorance is not knowing the nature of reality and clinging to the self. From this ignorance arises attachment, which is also called desire. Then comes anger, which is also called hatred. From these three main defilements arise jealousy, pride, and so on. Thus, the cause of suffering is these defilements of attachment, anger, ignorance, jealousy, and other impure thoughts, which arise from self-clinging.

Having these defilements, we undertake actions, or karma: physical actions, verbal actions, and mental actions. Creating karma is like planting seeds. Of course, there are negative actions and positive actions. Negative, or nonvirtuous, actions are actions that ripen as unpleasant experiences—pain and difficulty. It is like a tree with poisonous roots: everything that grows from it will be similarly poisonous. In the same way, any action arising from the defilements of ignorance, desire, and anger produces only suffering. And all such actions begin with clinging to a self.

Nonvirtuous actions of body, speech, and mind are often enumerated into ten types. The three nonvirtuous actions of the body are killing, stealing, and sexual misconduct. The four nonvirtuous actions of the voice are lies, speech that creates disharmony, harsh words that cause pain, and idle talk—talk that has no benefit and instead gives rise to defilements. The three nonvirtuous actions of the mind are covetousness, ill will, and wrong view, which means not believing in karma—the law of cause and effect. These are the ten nonvirtuous actions. Poverty, the inability to fulfill our wishes, anxiety, and all of the undesirable things that we face are the product of unwholesome and nonvirtuous actions that we committed in the past. Therefore, in order not to experience more pain in the future, we must avoid nonvirtuous actions now.

Whether Buddhist or non-Buddhist, no one wants to suffer. Nobody in any society, from tiny insects up to human beings, wants suffering. Everyone wants happiness, and everyone is running in pursuit of that happiness. Yet, although their aim is happiness, due to ignorance, they are constantly creating more causes for suffering. Such is the tragedy of ignorance. If you wish to be free of suffering and to accomplish happiness, you must understand the actual source of suffering, so that you can avoid the causes of suffering and accumulate the true causes of happiness.

The Buddha helps sentient beings not through the performance of great miracles or some kind of divine intervention but through his teachings. The Buddha taught that everything is created from our own actions. So if you commit wrongs, the Buddha cannot save you. Although the Buddha came to this world and displayed many different manifestations and accomplished many different actions, the biggest, the most important thing that he did was to give his teachings. He taught what is right and what is wrong. We must follow not the wrong way but the right way. Our future happiness depends upon it.

Liberation or enlightenment is entirely up to us. The Buddha said, "I have shown you the path of liberation." The Buddha cannot just give us liberation. The Buddha said, "I cannot wash away your sins with water; I cannot remove your suffering with my hand, like pulling

a thorn from your body. Neither can I transfer my realization to you."
The Buddha helps sentient beings by showing us the truth. If we
correctly follow this truth, because we have buddha nature, we have
the opportunity to attain liberation or enlightenment. As the Buddha
said, "You are your own savior." No one else can save us; only we can
save ourselves. This is one of the main differences between Buddhism
and other religions. Buddhists by and large believe that individual
effort is paramount. We need the Buddha's guidance of course, and
we rely on others in our Dharma training, but the main factor must
be our own efforts.

When we get sick, we need a skilled doctor and good medical facilities. But to get better, we must follow the doctor's advice—do the
right things, take the medicine, eat the right food, avoid the wrong
food, avoid the wrong behavior, and so on. By doing these things,
our sickness can be cured. Even if we have the best doctor and best
medical facilities, if we do not follow the doctor's advice, do not take
the medicine, and continuously eat the wrong food, we will not be
cured. The Buddha is like a doctor. The Dharma is like a medicine.
We ourselves are like patients. Our current defilements are like the
illness. To cure these defilements, we must take the right medicine.
That medicine is the Dharma that the Buddha taught: how to follow
the right path and how to avoid the wrong path.

The second truth is the truth of the cause, and the Buddha said
that we have to avoid these causes. Without avoiding the causes of
suffering, we cannot expect to overcome suffering. Just by praying to
the Buddha, or by wishing alone, we cannot overcome suffering. We
need to have real faith in the Buddha and then to follow his teachings
to avoid nonvirtuous deeds arising from defilements. Actions arising
from defilements are our closest enemies. No other enemy can create
such suffering. Our defilements can cause sufferings that we cannot
even imagine. The biggest enemy is not external; our biggest enemy
is actually within our own mind.

Realizing this, we must try to avoid and eliminate the defilements. It is not easy, of course, because we have associated with the defilements from beginningless time until now. It is no surprise that controlling anger, desire, jealousy, and so forth is so difficult. But the first step toward eliminating the defilements is realizing that the real cause of suffering is not our outside enemies; the real cause is actually our own inner defilements. It is because of these defilements, in fact, that we perceive outside enemies.

Outside enemies are like reflections in a mirror, reflections of our own image reflected back at us. Just as there is no one in the mirror apart from the reflected image of our own body, all of these outside problems, obstacles, enemies, and so on are the reflections of our own defilements. Therefore, if we control or destroy our inner defilements, all of our outer enemies and obstacles naturally disappear. This is the implication of the second truth, the truth of the cause.

These first two truths are actually the cause and result of samsara. First there is the truth of suffering, and then there is the truth of its cause. The Buddha gave the result first. Normally, the cause comes first and the result second, but the Buddha was very skillful in teaching the result first. For until we realize that life is suffering, we will not want to apply the remedy for suffering. Because nobody wants suffering, the Buddha pointed out the truth of our suffering first. To overcome that suffering, you have to avoid the cause, and that is what is explained in the second truth.

The Noble Truth of Cessation

The third truth is the truth of cessation. The state of cessation of suffering is called *nirvana*, or real peace. Nirvana is completely free of defilements. The attainment of nirvana is therefore complete peace.

Here again, in this second pair of truths, the result is given first, because when we see the benefit of the result, then we will wish to obtain it. Businesspeople, before investing in a new venture, will first see how much profit they can gain. If they do not see a profit, they will not pursue that business. By the same token, the Buddha first taught the truth of cessation, which is the result. On ceasing all defilements, we attain true peace and happiness. Once we truly realize how marvelous such a state would be, we will waste no effort in attaining that result.

The Noble Truth of the Path

To accomplish the truth of cessation, we must walk on the path. This last truth is called the *truth of the path*. When we long for the result, then of course we will naturally enter the truth of the path. This truth is the essence of the Buddha's teaching.

How do we enter the Buddha's path? The very first step is to take refuge in the Triple Gem—the Buddha, Dharma, and Sangha. You do not become a Buddhist just by being born into a Buddhist family. To become a Buddhist you must take refuge. Taking refuge is important because it is the root of all Dharma, the preliminary practice of all the paths, and the foundation of all vows. You cannot receive any Buddhist vows without first taking refuge.

Taking refuge is also what distinguishes Buddhists from non-Buddhists. What makes you a Buddhist is taking refuge in the Triple Gem, the Three Jewels. By this alone, you become a Buddhist. Someone may be a spiritual person, but without refuge in the Buddha, Dharma, and Sangha, he or she is not Buddhist. To be called a Buddhist, you must have taken the vow of refuge.

The Buddha, Dharma, and Sangha are the same in all Buddhist schools, whether Theravada, Mahayana, or Vajrayana, but the explanation in each differs slightly. Generally the word *buddha* means "fully enlightened one." According to the Mahayana teachings, a buddha is one who possesses the three *kayas*, or "bodies." The three bodies are the *dharmakaya*, the *sambhogakaya*, and the *nirmanakaya*. *Dharmakaya* means "body of reality," which can be thought of as wisdom, or the realization of ultimate truth.

Buddhists do not believe in a God who is a creator of everything, but Buddhists do believe in ultimate wisdom. This ultimate wisdom, the dharmakaya, is actually the basic wisdom, completely free of obscurations, that everyone possesses. Although we all have this basic wisdom, this buddha nature, at the moment our buddha nature is concealed by obscurations. In the case of a buddha's dharmakaya, every form of obscuration has been completely eliminated. It is known, therefore, as "doubly pure." Doubly because, first, it has the natural purity that we all possess, and second, because all temporary obscurations have also been eliminated.

The *sambhogakaya*, the "body of enjoyment," is the most exalted physical form of the buddhas. As these buddhas dwell in the buddhafields or pure lands, this form is visible only to the highest bodhisattvas, the most advanced followers of the Buddha.

The third body is called the *nirmanakaya*, which means "body of emanations." While the *sambhogakaya* always dwells in the buddhafields, a *nirmanakaya* is an emanation in ordinary form. It appears whenever, wherever, in whatever form is required according to the particular circumstances and needs of beings. The historical Buddha Shakyamuni, who attained enlightenment in India, was a *nirmanakaya*.

According to the Mahayana teachings, the Buddha had already attained enlightenment long before he came to India. He purposely chose to be born in a royal family, to become a renunciate, to search for the truth, to attain enlightenment under the bodhi tree in Bodhgaya, to give the teachings, and to eventually attain mahaparinirvana at Kushinagara. He did this to set an example of how an ordinary person like a prince can attain enlightenment and to show people how to search and work toward enlightenment.

The Buddha in whom we take refuge possesses all three *kayas*, has removed every form of obscuration, and has accomplished every possible good quality. To take a journey to an unknown place, you need an experienced guide who can show you the right path. The Buddha is the guide who shows us the path.

The second jewel in which we take refuge is the Dharma. The Sanskrit word *dharma* actually has many different meanings, even within Buddhism. But when we refer to the "holy Dharma," it has two aspects. The first aspect of the Dharma is the experience or realization of the buddhas and bodhisattvas. The second aspect is the teachings.

Buddhas and bodhisattvas put the experience and realization that they accomplish into words and offer them to sentient beings. This is called *turning the wheel of Dharma*. When a wheel turns, it gets us to our destination. In this case the wheel has two aspects: realization and teachings. The Buddha gave teachings about the knowledge and realization that he gained. As we work hard and gain this knowledge ourselves, we proceed further on the path and eventually attain liberation and enlightenment. That is to say, the more we hear the teachings, the more we understand. The more we understand, the more realization we have. The more realization we have, the closer we are to enlightenment. Because it turns through these stages, it is called the wheel of Dharma.

We take refuge in the Buddha as our guide to show us the right path, but we take refuge in the Dharma as the actual path. Because by practicing the Dharma ourselves, we proceed on the path. Therefore, the Dharma is our real savior, that which saves us from the suffering of samsara.

The third refuge is the *Sangha*, which means "community." The true Sangha, however, are those who are already on what is known as the *irreversible path*. These are bodhisattvas who have already reached a certain level from which they will never fall back into mundane cyclic existence again. These bodhisattvas are the real Sangha. But the Sangha more broadly are our companions in Dharma practice. When we must make a very long and difficult journey, it is better to have fellow travelers who are going to the same destination and the same way than to travel alone. The Sangha are our companions along the path.

So we start the Buddhist path by taking refuge in the Three Jewels: the Buddha, the Dharma, and the Sangha.

Buddhism has many different schools, but in general, there are two approaches: Hinayana and Mahayana. Hinayana primarily emphasizes attainment of nirvana—ultimate peace—for yourself. Life is suffering and nobody wants suffering. To eliminate this suffering, this school teaches you to renounce the world and attain nirvana for yourself. When all the fuel is exhausted, a fire is naturally extinguished. Similarly, when all the defilements are exhausted, suffering vanishes, and you naturally attain nirvana, which is the experience of complete peace and happiness.

In contrast, in the Mahayana, the goal is not nirvana for ourselves alone. Every sentient being has been here in the universe from beginningless time. In all this time here, we have taken countless lives in myriad forms. There is not a single place where we have not been born. There is not a single sentient being who has not at one time been our parent or relative. Even in this life, our whole existence depends on others, on our parents, our teachers, our friends, our companions. So to seek liberation for ourselves alone is not right.

Even from a worldly perspective, if we alone are safe and enjoying great pleasures but the rest of our family is in great suffering, if we are goodhearted people, we will not be happy. From this, we can recognize that it is not right to seek happiness or liberation just for ourselves. We need to consider the welfare of all sentient beings.

Every sentient being has been our very dear mother, father, or relative, but because of the trauma of the process of death and rebirth, we do not recognize each other. We see some as our friends, we see others as enemies, and toward some we are indifferent. But in reality, every sentient being is our very dear one. Therefore, we must repay the benefit and kindness that they have given us. The best way to pay this back is to rescue them from the suffering of samsara and to place them on the path to enlightenment. Therefore, we seek enlightenment for the benefit of every living being without any exception.

To seek enlightenment for the benefit of every living being is the Mahayana path. This is the greatest path. It is of great merit to benefit even one sentient being. If our goal is to benefit countless, limitless sentient beings, then that is of infinite benefit. The resolve to attain enlightenment for the benefit of all beings is called *enlightenment mind*, or *bodhichitta*.

To give rise to this enlightenment mind, we must develop loving kindness and compassion. Loving kindness is like a mother's love for her child. Every mother wants her child to be happy, healthy, and to have good fortune and success. Similarly, we want every sentient being to be happy and to have the cause of happiness. Such a thought is called *loving kindness*.

When we have loving kindness, compassion naturally arises. *Compassion* is the wish that every sentient being may be free from suffering and the cause of suffering. If we examine reality carefully, we will find that no sentient being is truly happy, and in fact, every sentient being is in the midst of suffering. They long for happiness, but out of ignorance, they create more and more causes of suffering. It is on this basis that we generate compassion for them.

From loving kindness and compassion, enlightenment mind arises. Enlightenment mind, again, is defined as the resolution to attain ultimate enlightenment so that one may be of greatest benefit of all sentient beings, just like Shakyamuni Buddha himself. The Buddha also first generated enlightenment mind, then accumulated wisdom and merit, and eventually attained enlightenment, through which he benefited countless sentient beings.

We are followers of the Buddha, and particularly we are Mahayanists. We must cultivate not only the abandonment of nonvirtuous deeds and defilements but also the accumulation of loving kindness, compassion, and enlightenment mind. In this way, we will be able to attain enlightenment for the sake of all sentient beings.

This concludes my short explanation of the essence of the Buddha's teachings. I hope it has inspired you to cultivate these teachings in your own life and so discover the fruits for yourself.

PART TWO

Developing Compassion

Mahasiddha Virupa with Krishnapa (left) and Vajra Nairatmya (right).
Photograph by John Bigelow Taylor, courtesy of the Kronos Collection.

The second part of this volume focuses on compassion—the foundation of Buddhism and the basis for developing enlightenment mind. The teachings in this section explain how to develop compassion through meditation. Matchless Compassion, by the great Indian saint and scholar Virupa, is a well-known teaching by one of the masters most important to the Sakya lineage. The text explains how to develop compassion toward all sentient beings and especially enemies, for whom it is difficult for ordinary people to feel compassion.

This section begins with a biography of Virupa. In Tibetan Buddhism, it is traditional to begin study of a text by first learning the life story of the master who taught it. Although Virupa lived during the seventh to eighth centuries, his teachings remain highly applicable today. His life story shows the extent to which he mastered both great compassion and great wisdom. It is filled with inspiring illustrations of how his great compassion enabled him to handle those who tried to harm him.

After studying Virupa's biography, study the root text that he taught and then the explanation of it. Then contemplate them until you can remember and understand them clearly. Try to mix the teachings with your mind and repeatedly practice the meditations described. These are the very same meditation practices that have been used by great Indian and Tibetan masters for more than a thousand years.

The Life Story of Mahasiddha Virupa

Jetsun Dragpa Gyaltsen (1147–1216)

I BOW MY HEAD at the feet of the holy lamas!

The lord of mahasiddhas known as Virupa was born to an Indian royal family sometime during the seventh and eighth centuries. He completely abandoned his kingdom and went to Nalanda University. He was ordained as a monk by the abbot Dharmamitra and received the ordination name of Shri Dharmapala from this abbot, who also gave him empowerments and instruction on how to meditate on the deity Chakrasamvara.

Shri Dharmapala intensively studied the entire philosophy of his own and other schools and became an extremely learned monk. After his abbot, Dharmamitra, passed away, Shri Dharmapala became the greatest abbot among all the scholars of Nalanda University. He also continued his practice of Chakrasamvara. Although he practiced Chakrasamvara for a very long time, no positive signs of meditative attainment arose, and in fact, various unpleasant signs occurred. Discouraged, he resolved that from then on, he would only teach Dharma, compose texts, and lead the Sangha and would discontinue his practice of Chakrasamvara.

On the twenty-second of the fourth lunar month, known as the month of Vaishakha, Shri Dharmapala threw his *mala* rosary in the toilet and relaxed his activities. That same night, Vajra Nairatmya appeared in his dream as an ordinary lady of bluish color. She spoke to him saying, "Son of my lineage, such an inappropriate act was not well done. Retrieve your mala and wash it with scented water. Confess and commit yourself to right practice. I am the deity with whom you have a karmic connection. I will bless you, and you will swiftly reach attainment." Speaking thus, she disappeared.

Shri Dharmapala awoke, his mind filled with regret. The next day, on the twenty-third, he retrieved his mala and did as she had commanded. That night, he perceived the primordial wisdom emanation body of Vajra Nairatmya with a retinue of fifteen goddesses, and they bestowed upon him profound and complete initiation, empowering him into their mandala. During the empowerment, the primordial wisdom of the path of seeing arose in his mind, which is the stage of a bodhisattva of the first level (*bhumi*). Similarly, his realization advanced successively each night until the night of the twenty-ninth, when he reached the realization of the sixth level. In this way, the stream of empowerment from the Buddha Vajradhara to Virupa was unbroken. Through the arising of realization from the first to the sixth bhumis, the stream of blessings did not decline.

Earlier, when the lack of clear signs of attainment was followed by many unpleasant signs, Shri Dharmapala had become discouraged with practice. These were the signs of the heat of meditation, yet he did not recognize them as such because he had not received the necessary explanations from experienced teachers. Once he reached the sixth level of realization, he then fully understood the significance of these occurrences, which showed that the sequence of instructions he had followed had been unmistaken.

With that, he attained genuine definitive understanding that his realization was equal to that of a perfectly and fully enlightened buddha, as a result of which his devotion did not decline. Through these, he was both blessed by the four oral instructions and taught by the four oral instructions, which means that he had received the essential requirements of the complete teaching of the *Lamdre* or "Path and Result."

Shri Dharmapala continued to meditate on his realization and remained in his room. Some people noticed him bringing meat and liquor there and peered through cracks in the doors. Some perceived him to be sitting with fifteen ladies, and others perceived him to be sitting with eight ladies. Some perceived him to be sitting with fifteen burning oil lamps, and others perceived him to be sitting with eight burning oil lamps. After seeing these various things, others began to doubt him, yet Shri Dharmapala could be neither accused nor expelled, because he was the highest abbot among all the scholars.

At that time, in order to defend the pure discipline of the holy doctrine as beyond reproach, Shri Dharmapala thought, "I should declare that I have been improper." He left his room and offered his begging bowl, Dharma robes, and other monastic possessions before the holy shrine. He declared, "*Ame virupa* (My body is unattractive)!" and, naked, departed directly.

Having left monastic life, he adopted the name Virupa. He begged some flowers from flower sellers, fashioned them into garlands, and wore them around his head. He begged some leaves and radishes, put some in his mouth, and carried the rest in his hands. He went to bars and houses of prostitution, astonishing everyone by his behavior.

At Nalanda, the monastic community was summoned by the beating of gongs and drums. They proceeded to expel him from the monastery and resolved that he would not be allowed to return. At that time, Virupa sang songs of religious experience that are preserved in other texts.

To benefit Lord Buddha's doctrine, to avert the disrespect of the worldly toward himself, and to symbolically demonstrate that his actions were improper, when Virupa approached the sacred Ganges River on his journey toward Varanasi, he said, "I am an improper person, so give me a path by which to cross [so that I do not defile the river]." At that moment, the great river stopped flowing, and the stream parted, providing a path for him to cross. After that, Virupa sang a song of his religious experience.

Through these actions, the Sangha realized that Virupa had achieved high attainment. They prostrated at his feet, begged his forgiveness, offered their apologies, and requested him to remain at the university. He accepted their apology but not their request to stay.

Virupa traveled about in the forests of Varanasi and abided there for a long time without clothing or other possessions. From exposure to the sun and air, his body became very frightening, and he looked like a wandering ascetic. As such, some believed that he was a Hindu yogi, while others believed that he was a Buddhist yogi.

After a while, the Hindu king of Varanasi declared, "If that yogi is Hindu, he has endured many hardships, and so we should invite him to the palace. If he is Buddhist, it may not be good for the people of Varanasi. Everyone, try to find out what his religion is." The people watched him but could not find any signs indicating his religion. Finally, the king summoned Virupa before him.

Virupa came in response to the summons, along the way catching flies and moths and putting them in his mouth. The people told him, "You are improper," so by his great meditative attainments, he revived the flies and moths, but still they complained, "You are improper." Then the great master said, "If I kill sentient beings, you say that I am improper. If I revive them, you say that I am improper. I don't know how to behave!"

Virupa came before the king. The king asked him again and again, "Who are you?" but Virupa made no reply whatsoever. Finally, the king said, "There is no indication that this man is a Hindu or a follower of Shiva. Chain his arms and legs and throw him in the river." The people did as the king instructed, but the great yogi returned to the palace and again appeared before the king. Again and again they tried but were completely unsuccessful. Through these acts, the local people were converted to follow him on the Vajrayana path.

Then Virupa went south, to tame Bhimeshvara (Tib. *Bi me sa ra*). On the way, when Virupa again reached the Ganges River, he asked a sailor to ferry him to the other side. The sailor asked for the fare, but the great master replied, "I will satisfy you. If I give you the river, will that be sufficient?" First the sailor answered that he wanted more than the river. Then he said that he wanted less than that. The master said, "I will give you the river itself," and pointed at the river with a threatening mudra. The Ganges River reversed, and many people who lived in huts on the banks were terrified that they would be carried away by the flood.

The sailor told the people, "That man caused this." Everyone was terrified. Some people brought jewels, others brought gold, others brought silver, others brought cattle, others brought piles of grain, and still others brought flower garlands, all requesting Virupa to let the water flow. Virupa snapped his fingers, and the water flowed as normal. Then he sang a song of his religious experience. The great yogi gave all of the offerings to the sailor, saying, "This is your fare."

The sailor clutched the master's feet and begged, "I don't want any of these things. Please let me follow you, and accept me as your disciple." The great yogi accepted his request, and the sailor followed him. They returned all of the offerings to the people who had given them.

From there, they went south to Dakinipata, near Bhimeshvara. There, they went to a beer shop and asked to purchase some beer. The owner asked them, "What will you give me for it?"

The master replied, "If you satisfy me, I will give whatever you desire."

Not trusting him, the owner asked, "When will you pay me?"

The master drew a line saying, "I will pay you when the sun's shadow passes this point."

The master then held the sun beneath his heel while asking the owner to bring more and more beer. When all the beer in the shop was gone, the owner demanded payment, but Virupa said, "The sun has not yet reached this point. Bring more beer." In this way, the master drank all the beer from eighteen valleys.

Meanwhile, the king and the other people in the city became completely confused about what time it was, and everyone became drunk from exhaustion and sleepiness. The king, learning that a yogi was demonstrating his power, asked Virupa to let the sun go.

The master replied, "I have nothing with which to pay for this beer." The king paid the beer seller the price of the beer, after which the great master released the sun, and it immediately became midnight. Virupa sang a song of his religious realization, and his fame spread wherever the rays of the sun shown.

From there, Virupa went south to Bhimeshvara, a Shiva lingam made of clay. At that place there lived five hundred long-haired heretic yogis, whom the master intended to bring on to the Buddhist path. Upon his arrival, Virupa elegantly spoke many praises of their king in the Sanskrit language. The king was pleased and appointed Virupa the leader of the five hundred yogis, making royal offerings to him. Nevertheless, the great master continued his own practices, making offerings of flowers and prostrations to the Perfection of Wisdom (Prajnaparamita) text that he carried with him and never once prostrating to the Shiva shrine. Seeing this, everyone began to doubt him, and they reported the situation to the king. The king said, "It is impossible that he does not prostrate to the shrine—he is extremely learned in Sanskrit, and I appointed him the leader of the five hundred yogis. You are merely jealous," and ignored them.

Again and again, however, others reported the same thing, and at a certain point, the king began to doubt. The king invited the master with all the yogis and ordered all of them to prostrate to the Shiva shrine. All of the yogis prostrated to the shrine, but the master prostrated to his text. Then the king ordered Virupa to prostrate to the Shiva shrine, but the master replied, "I cannot prostrate to the shrine because the shrine cannot endure it."

The king said, "Shiva is the highest god in the desire realm, so how could the shrine not endure it? You must prostrate."

The master said, "O god, this sinful king forces me to prostrate, so I apologize if you cannot endure it."

Thus saying, the great master put his right palm on his forehead and said, "Namo Buddhaya." The top third of the Shiva lingam cracked. Placing his hand at his throat he said, "Namo Dharmaya," and the second third of the lingam cracked. Placing his hand at his heart he said, "Namo Sanghaya," and the lingam cracked completely. Then he repeated this from each of the four directions, and the lingam completely broke into four pieces.

The king and the entire gathering were completely terrified and grasped his feet in supplication. The master reassembled the pieces of the lingam and put a black stone image of Avalokiteshvara, the bodhisattva of great compassion, on top of it. He advised them, "From now on, prostrate, offer, and circumambulate this shrine. If you remove the image of the Great Compassionate One (Mahakarunika) or cease to prostrate and make offerings to it, the shrine will be destroyed."

Thus advising them, he continued his journey south. At the time of Virupa's departure, he was followed by one of the five hundred yogis who became known as Krishnapa. On Virupa's journey south, Buddha statues or stupas were put on top of all the Hindu shrines, out of fear that he might otherwise destroy them. Seeing this, he was delighted, thinking, "Even my name has served Lord Buddha's doctrine."

Reaching the south, there was a Shiva statue made of red wood known as Tambra Pratima to which people sacrificed hundreds of buffalo at a time. Approaching the statue, Virupa kicked its feet saying, "Get out of here." The statue moved and then followed the great master. All the heretics were terrified and begged him not to take the statue. The master replied, "If you promise not to sacrifice buffalo and instead offer rice and other things, I will allow it to remain. Otherwise I will not." The people promised accordingly, and he returned the statue to its place.

From there, Virupa traveled east to Sahaja Devi, where there was a naturally arisen trident and a naturally arisen stone statue of the wrathful heretic deity Chandika. There, heretic yogis tricked people and lured them inside, where the naturally arisen trident speared their necks and they died, after which the yogis feasted on their flesh. When the master Virupa and his two attendants approached the place, the heretic yogis wanted to eat them and invited them inside the shrine.

The master advised his attendants, "Hold your breath and do not exhale. Stay outside." The master alone entered the shrine.

The yogis asked, "Where are your two companions?"

He replied, "They are outside."

The yogis said, "Ask them to come in, too."

Virupa replied, "You go ask them."

The yogis went outside to invite them inside. Neither replied to the invitation, so the yogis poked them with their fingers and heard the sound of flatulence and saw excrement expelled. They said, "Both of them are already rotten," and returned inside the shrine.

Suddenly, the trident began to shake and the master clapped his hands, smashing it to dust and ashes. Then the statue of Chandika rose up, and the master slammed its head in, pushing it all the way down to its heart. The master held the statue's ear and put a stupa on its head. All the yogis fainted.

When they revived, the yogis said to the master, "How could you do this? You are a Buddhist and are supposed to be compassionate."

The master advised them, "Do not make offerings of the warm flesh and blood of slaughtered beings."

The yogis prostrated at the feet of the master and took refuge, and all became Buddhist. At that moment, the master Virupa blessed the mind of his sailor attendant and gave him complete instruction, such that his realization became equal to the master. Then Virupa sent his disciple to the east to subjugate the heretic King Dehara. Virupa's unsurpassable spiritual power was proclaimed throughout the land.

Next, Virupa with his attendant from among the southern yogis went to circumambulate the shrine of Avalokiteshvara. There, the great master offered his realization, beginning with his entry into the door of Buddhism, up to his subjugation of Sahaja Devi, describing before the statue of greatly compassionate Avalokiteshvara each of the activities that he had performed for Lord Buddha's doctrine.

Avalokiteshvara said to him, "Son of my lineage, through your power, even mountains could be turned to ash. Yet sentient beings have such manifold karma that it is difficult for even the buddhas to tame all of them. From now on, do not use violent actions toward beings, and generate great compassion for them."

The master replied, "I will do no more, but one. In the west, at Somanatha, is a naturally arisen Shiva lingam. Thousands of buffalo at a time are slaughtered there as offerings. To save beings' lives, I shall subjugate those adherents. After that, I will follow your advice, O Great Compassionate One."

Avalokiteshvara spoke to him, "Still, do not destroy the shrine. Tame them through skillful methods."

Then the master and his attendant set out for the west. On the way, they made prostrations and circumambulations at many Buddhist shrines. Shiva realized that the master was approaching and emanated two brahmans wearing skirts made of *krishnasara* deerskin and with pieces of *kusha* grass behind their ears to identify them as brahmans.

The brahmans greeted the master and asked him, "Where are you going?"

The master replied, "I am going to destroy Somanatha."

The brahmans said, "You Buddhists are supposed to be compassionate. Why use such violence?"

The master replied, "That's exactly why I'm going. Because thousands of buffalo are sacrificed every day, I'm going to destroy the shrine."

The brahmans asked, "Can you destroy it? The god is the greatest in the world."

The master said, "We will see what happens."

The brahmans said, "The god is not here. He already departed toward the east."

The master said, "No matter where he goes, in any of the four directions, even if he goes to the Brahma realm, I will go there, too, and destroy him."

Then Shiva actually manifested in front of the master and prostrated to his feet, saying, "I am he, and I will do what you say."

The master instructed him, "In that case, build a temple with an image of the Buddha in it, below it put an image of me, and provide the necessities for a hundred monks to live at that monastery. When making offerings, offer the first portion to the Buddha, the second portion to me, and the third portion to yourself, making offerings of only rice, flowers, fruit, and bread. If you do this, I will not destroy you. If you do not do it, I will destroy you." The master spoke thus, and the god promised to follow his instructions.

The god requested of the master, "As long as Somanatha remains, please also remain to accept our offerings."

Virupa's disciple's realization was not quite equal to the master's. Virupa blessed him so that they would become equal and gave him the *Vajra Verses*. He advised him to go east and benefit sentient beings through the Vajrayana teaching.

The master himself remained in Somanatha, in accord with the god's request. Meanwhile, he ceased his activities of taming beings through violence. Some say that Virupa absorbed his body into the statue. Others say that the statue is Virupa himself. The statue is known to still remain, and will remain as long as the sun and moon abide.

Other explanations state, "When the name Virupa appears in the center of India, one known as Elephant Sunrise will be tamed and quarrels will occur, but beings will be benefitted. I will also reappear once to tame Bhimeshvara."

In any case, through his spiritual power, the lord of mahasiddhas Virupa spread the Buddha's doctrine and tamed heretics as explained herein. He received empowerment directly from the emanation body of the primordial wisdom dakini with a retinue of fifteen goddesses, and he was blessed through the four oral instructions, the unbroken stream of empowerment, and the rest, as previously explained.

Likewise, Virupa blessed Krishnapa from the east; who blessed the great yogi Damarupa from central India; who blessed Avadhutipa, who relinquished both extremes; who blessed Gayadhara, who was from the caste of royal scribes in the east and attained stable realization of creation, was able to perceive emanation deities, could place the vajra and bell in space, and could project his mind into other bodies without hindrance. Gayadhara blessed Jetsun Mikyo Dorje, who blessed She dang Dorje, who blessed Rolpai Dorje, who blessed the Great Sakyapa Mikyo Dorje. In this way, instruction occurred through the four oral instructions, and they were blessed through the four oral instructions.

This was written by the lord of yogis, Dragpa Gyaltsen.

> The Sangha did not investigate whether noble or not and,
> beating drums and gongs, showed that the improper one
>   should go.
> My stainless mind is hard to realize, like the moon.
> So I am Virupa, owner of many sciences.

> Split the terrifying lingam, terrifying even the foundation.
> Virupa drank beer and held the sun beneath his heel.
> Like an utpala remained unaffected by water.
> So I am Virupa, owner of many sciences.

Stopped the stream of the Ganges then let it flow again.
Like an utpala remained unaffected by water.
Profound stainless mind hard to realize.
So I am Virupa, owner of many sciences.

Worldly ones, worldly ones, be not deluded by ignorance!
Worldly ones, worldly ones, be not confused by beer!
If I wish, my mind holds the sun beneath my heel.
So I am Virupa, owner of many sciences.

Ithi!

From the *Collected Works of the Sakya Tradition*, volume *cha*, first volume of
the *Collected Works of Dragpa Gyaltsen*, work number 11. Translated and edited
by Khenpo Kalsang Gyaltsen and Ani Kunga Chodron at Sakya Phuntsok Ling
near Washington, DC. By this merit, may all beings reach the stage of Mahasiddha Virupa.

Training the Mind in Matchless Compassion: Pith Instructions of the Glorious Virupa

COMPILED BY MUCHEN SEMPA CHENPO KONCHOG GYALTSEN (1388–1469)

Namo Ratna Guru!
The glorious Virupa stated:

> Meditate on compassion toward those who are kind
> because they have cared for you kindly since beginningless time.
> Those who harm you now are your mothers,
> and in the past they benefited you repeatedly.
> Lacking self-control, like the deranged,
> they will fall into Avici hell through their negative acts.
> By recollecting this of all beings in the three worlds of
>   existence,
> compassion will be accomplished.

EXPLANATION OF THE MEDITATION ON MATCHLESS COMPASSION

Compassion is the root of the Mahayana Dharma. Without compassion, practice of the six perfections and the Vajrayana commitments of creation and completion, along with every other Dharma act, will belong to the lower vehicle. Kindness, compassion, and

Muchen Sempa Chenpo Konchog Gyaltsen (1388–1469),
the second abbot of Ngor Ewam Monastery.
Collection of the Rubin Museum of Art. Himalayan Art Resources 368.

enlightenment mind are absolutely necessary. "Kindness" means to benefit others.

Begin your meditation upon compassion with those who cause you harm. Sit in meditation posture in a secluded place. Take refuge and generate enlightenment mind. Visualize that you yourself are the tutelary deity and that your guru sits above the crown of your head.

Directly in front of you, visualize those enemies who cause you the most serious harm. In your meditation, alternate between a continuous stream of compassion and the reasons for that compassion. First, physically, make an effort to sit in the proper posture. Mentally, concentrate single-pointedly on those who harm you. Verbally, recite "Poor them, who cause harm to me." Recite this a hundred, fifty, or twenty-one times. Meditate on this continuous stream of compassion. Second, understand that this agent of harm was your own mother in previous lives. Therefore, repeat many times, "Poor them! How worthy of compassion this person is!"

Why should you feel compassion toward this enemy? One reason is that the enemy has been your mother not only once or twice but many times. Think thus and recite "Poor them!" many times.

Again, why should you feel compassion toward this enemy? Another reason is that each time they were your mother, they provided boundless benefits. Think thus and recite "Poor them!" many times.

And again, why should you feel compassion toward this enemy? Generally, a mother is someone who benefits you. If she is supposed to be benefiting me, why is she now causing me harm? Although this agent of harm was once my mother, she is now unable to control her own mind, like a deranged person. Therefore, she harms other sentient beings in general and her own children in particular. Think thus and recite "Poor her!" many times.

Once more, why should you feel compassion toward this enemy? Because this enemy causes harm, he or she will fall into the Avici or other hells and will be tormented by terrible suffering. Think thus and recite "Poor them!" many times.

Meditate thus, alternating between concentration, repetition, and thinking about the reasons for compassion.

While doing this, tears may fall from your eyes, your hair may stand on end, and other physical signs of unbearable feelings may arise. If such signs occur, then genuine compassion has been generated, and you should think, "I must achieve perfect enlightenment, buddhahood, for the benefit of all sentient beings, primarily these agents of harm." Then wish that all sentient beings and these agents of harm attain the stage of tutelary deities. After that, meditate for a long time in the state of primordial wisdom free of elaboration. If a cloud of conceptual thoughts arises, then dedicate the merit and conclude the session.

Thus, in the same way as before, expand whatever compassion you can develop toward one being to other beings by meditating on those who cause moderate and lesser harm.

Then meditate on those who are family and relatives, and then on beings in your locality, region, and country, as well as those on the four continents, the three thousand worlds of existence, and finally every single being stretching to the limits of space. Your compassion, pervading everywhere, thus becomes infinite.

Doing this meditation helps to pacify anger and other negative emotions. It also helps to pacify any negative conditions: evil spirits, illness, leprosy, and the like.

Changing the mind in this way develops compassion toward all sentient beings as if each were your only child, and as a result, genuine primordial wisdom free of elaboration will arise.

MEDITATION ON THE ROOT CAUSE

When the intellect is disturbed by unruly beings and inner
   and outer activities,

remember enlightenment mind and the exchange of self and
   other.
Through it, conquer the host of maras and defilements,
and transform them into primordial wisdom free of elaboration.

This explains that the cause of achieving omniscience is enlightenment mind (*bodhichitta*). There are two types of enlightenment mind:
relative and ultimate. Of these two, the latter is ultimate primordial
wisdom free of elaboration.

Concerning the first, relative enlightenment mind, although there
are many practices, gurus most often explain the practice of exchanging self and other. In this practice, when severe physical illness, mental
sorrow, or both occur, or when external sufferings such as enemies or
evil spirits arise, or when internal sufferings such as imbalances in the
elements, excessive defilements, and so forth arise, at that moment
take that suffering onto the path.

For instance, if a strong angry thought arises, think, "By this angry
thought of mine, may all the causes and results of the angry thoughts
of all sentient beings who harbor serious anger ripen upon me."

Also think, "May whatever suffering in the minds of sentient beings,
which is the result of defilements and is produced by self-clinging,
ripen upon me. Particularly, may the sufferings of hell, such as being
burned and cooked in the fires of hell; the starvation and thirst of
hungry ghosts; the killing and exploitation of animals; the fighting
and quarreling of demigods; the falling from luxury of the gods; and
the birth, aging, illness, and death of human beings; as well as the illnesses of the sick, the destitution of the poor, and the suffering of the
handicapped and crippled all ripen upon me. May all hindrances that
obstruct obtaining a human body with leisure and endowments and
obstruct moving through the paths and stages ripen upon my angry
thoughts."

Think thus one-pointedly and make efforts with your body, voice, and mind to gather the suffering of every sentient being and take it upon yourself. Meditate thus one-pointedly for one, two, or three hours or more. Think thus until the defilements of conceptual thoughts and the sufferings of disease are pacified. Verbally recite, "May the sufferings of all sentient beings ripen upon me."

Visualize that, as a result of your virtues amassed through the accumulations of merit and wisdom, rays of light shine forth from your heart and touch each and every sentient being. All sentient beings are placed upon the stage of tutelary deities, and their natures are that of a buddha's holy body and wisdom. Then rest the mind in the state of genuine primordial wisdom free of elaboration. If a cloud of conceptual thoughts arises, dedicate the merit and conclude the session. Beginners should practice thus.

After becoming familiar with this meditation, meditate in the same manner toward greater or lesser sufferings and fears.

Meditate one-pointedly and verbally recite, "By my virtues, may they all attain happiness."

Also think, "May my body, wealth, and virtues ripen upon all sentient beings, and may all of them attain uncontaminated happiness."

Although this meditation can be done slowly or swiftly, there is no difference in actual result. There are no differences in actual fact. Then, if conceptual thoughts arise, dedicate the merit and conclude the session.

By the power of relative enlightenment mind, in the beginning stages, you will become able to benefit other sentient beings, conceptual thoughts and defilements will be pacified, illness and evil spirits will be overcome, and you will attain a natural sovereignty. Ultimately, you will attain the result of the stages of the sambhogakaya and nirmanakaya and thereby become able to accomplish magnificent benefit for other beings. The seed of the dharmakaya will be planted by the power of ultimate enlightenment mind, and the excellent stage of mahamudra will be attained.

If these causes and conditions are gathered, various signs and marks will arise upon the body, voice, and mind. Particularly, the mind will be free of the characterization of subject and object, and it will produce calm abiding and insight meditation. This is known as the single-moment self-awareness of primordial wisdom.

In that single-moment self-awareness of primordial wisdom, you abide in the five primordial wisdoms in which the emptiness of nonconceptual mind is the dharmakaya, self-awareness is the sambhogakaya, luminosity is the nirmanakaya, and the indivisibility of the intrinsic nature of these three is the svabhavakaya. At this point, cognition free of elaboration is the primordial wisdom of the dharmadhatu, realization of the emptiness of self is mirror-like primordial wisdom, self-awareness is the primordial wisdom of discrimination, clarity is all-accomplishing primordial wisdom, and the indivisibility of these is the primordial wisdom of equality.

> By the genuine virtues that arise from this,
> with genuine enlightenment mind, emptiness, and compassion,
> may I swiftly place all sentient beings dwelling in samsara
> in the state of uncontaminated happiness.

These intentions of the glorious Virupa were taught by Darpana Acharya and are an explanatory text of Lowo Lotsawa. The lineage lamas of this pith instruction on matchless compassion are Vajradhara, Virupa, Lord Dombipa, Lord Mathipa, Yogi Nimkalamka, Lord Ravinthapa, Chag Lotsawa Chogye Pal, Lama Zhonnu Gyaltsen, Vajradhara Mathi Shri, Lama Yesheshab, Zangpo Pal, Buddharatna, Kirtishila, Jayabhadra, Punyeratna, and Zhonu Gyalchog. I [Muchen Konchog Gyaltsen] received it from that master.

His Holiness the Forty-First Sakya Trizin.
Photo by Clive Arrowsmith.

Vajradhara, Vajra Nairatmya, Virupa, and Krishnapa,
the first four masters of the Lamdre lineage.

From the collection of Barbara and Walter Frey.

Sachen Kunga Nyingpo, Sonam Tsemo, Dragpa Gyaltsen, and
Sakya Pandita, the first four of the five founders of the Sakya school.
Collection of Shelley and Donald Rubin. Himalayan Art Resources 203.

Muchen Sempa Chenpo Konchog Gyaltsen and Gorampa Sonam Senge.
Collection of the Rubin Museum of Art. Himalayan Art Resources 368.

An Explanation of Matchless Compassion

His Holiness Sakya Trizin

THIS TEACHING, given by the great Mahasiddha Virupa, is a method of training the mind to develop compassion.

VIRUPA

The great being who later became known as Virupa was born as a prince in the eastern part of India. His father, the king, was named Golden Wheel, so his son, the prince, was named Silver Wheel. When the prince was born, he possessed very special qualities and was quite different from ordinary people. He was naturally full of love and compassion, respected elders, and was kindhearted toward the poor and needy. In particular, he had a clear intention and strong desire to practice the Dharma.

As he grew up, Silver Wheel realized that samsara has no essence and that it is without genuine pleasure or happiness. Thus, although he was a prince, from a very young age he renounced his position and became a monk. He stayed in the temple and studied the scriptures. In order to further his studies, he felt it necessary to travel from the eastern part of India to the center of India, where at that time there were two very large and famous Buddhist monastic universities known as Vikramashila and Nalanda.

After Virupa came to Nalanda Monastery, he studied for many years under a great abbot and became very learned. From the abbot he received Vajrayana teachings on the tantric deity Shri Chakrasamvara. He practiced Chakrasamvara privately at night, and during the daytime he was occupied with giving public teachings, debating, and composing. Through these scholarly activities he helped thousands of monks and devotees.

But because he was secretly practicing the highest Chakrasamvara meditations at night, he expected to have certain signs of accomplishment. Yet after many years he still had no significant signs. Instead, he had many unpleasant signs, both in his dreams and in his waking experience. He thought, "Maybe I do not have a karmic connection with the Vajrayana teachings."

So he discontinued the Vajrayana teachings and gave up the practice, wishing to devote the remaining part of his life to scholarly activities and Mahayana meditations. But, on that very night, a blue lady appeared in his dream and said, "My son, what you did is not right. It is not that you do not have a karmic connection with the Vajrayana path. I am your karmic-link deity. I will accept you as my disciple, and I will give you the attainments." So he resumed his meditation. Again that very night, deities appeared in person and gave him the necessary empowerments and instructions, so that within one week he swiftly accomplished all the stages up to the sixth bodhisattva bhumi.

At that point, he had already gone beyond the worldly path. Having reached the stage of the sixth bhumi, he knew that the time was ripe to act in an extraordinary way, beyond common perception. So, instead of being the abbot of the monastery, he left the monastery and became a mahasiddha, a great tantric yogi. Through his enormous miracles, he propagated the Buddhadharma and benefited sentient beings. Of course, the main teaching that he gave is the Path and Result, or *Lamdre* teaching. The root text of the Lamdre teaching is known as the *Vajra Verses*. It was one of his main practices. Hevajra, the deity and tantra upon which the Lamdre teaching is based, was his main deity.

Virupa had another practice. In a way, it could be said that he gave two pith instructions. One is the *Vajra Verses*, the root text of the Lamdre teaching, and the other is known as the *Inactive Vajra Verses*. Actually, the main part of the teaching of the *Inactive Vajra Verses* is Vajrayana, or secret tantric teachings. But as a preliminary, it has special mind-training instructions related to compassion. For the present book, these mind-training instructions on compassion have been extracted and offered as a preliminary. Now I will give this teaching.

MOTIVATION

Of course, whenever we receive teachings, the very first thing is to establish a proper motivation, because it is motivation that creates the different levels of the spiritual path. Many people just come to listen to the Dharma out of curiosity, to gain knowledge, or even without any sort of driving purpose or motivation. Such motivations are not suitable.

Some people come to receive teachings just to overcome obstacles in this life. There are so many shortcomings in life, such as ill health, poverty, loss of opportunities, and so on. If we receive teachings for the sake of this life—in order to have a healthy life, a happy life, a wealthy life, a comfortable life, and so on—it is also not right, for as it says in *Parting from the Four Attachments*, "If you are attached to this life, you are not a religious person." In other words, the purpose of the Dharma is not to gain wealth, health, and so on in this life, but rather the purpose of the Dharma is to liberate us from samsara, from the cycle of existence. Therefore, to receive teachings motivated by the wish to overcome obstacles in this life is not right; there are other ways to attain such goals.

Now, some people think that this life is crucially important. But one day we have to leave this world. When we leave this world, although our physical body will be disposed of in one way or another, the mental consciousness, the mind, is something that can't be cremated and can't be buried. The mind is something we can't see with our naked eyes, something we can't touch with our hands, something we can't describe in terms of size or color or specific shape. Although the body will change, the mind cannot disappear; it has to go on. The mind can't be disposed of the way we dispose of our physical body.

If we have committed negative deeds, then we will fall down into the lower realms, which contain immense suffering. Fearing the lower realms, we may strive to be continuously reborn in the higher realms, such as in the human realm or in the god realms. If we listen to teachings or undertake practice with this motivation, it is a spiritual path— it is a Dharma path—because it transcends attachment to the present life. Nonetheless it is not a higher path, because the goal is still within the cycle of existence. To wish to be born continuously as a human being and to continue worldly existence is an inferior path.

Now, some people realize that not only in the lower realms, but even in the higher realms, there is no real happiness. We may feel there is happiness, there may appear to be happiness, but it is not truly happiness. As we can see if we investigate, in the human realm there is no lasting satisfaction. No one is one hundred percent happy. In the East or West, North or South, wherever you go, whatever you do, whether you have wealth or don't have wealth, no one is one hundred percent satisfied. The same is true of the gods and demigods.

This shows that samsara is not happy. Everywhere, not only in the lower realms, but also even in the highest god realm, and also in the human realm, everywhere, we find that there is no real happiness. In order to permanently overcome suffering, you need to liberate yourself from samsara completely. To do this, you need to attain nirvana. Motivated in this way, you strive to receive these teachings for the purpose of accomplishing total liberation or nirvana for yourself. This kind of Dharma motivation is a very great thing. Still it is not the highest motivation, and so it is called an intermediate person's path.

Not only is samsara full of suffering, but every sentient being is intimately connected to us. Since we have been caught up in samsara from beginningless time until now, we have changed our physical body many, many times, like changing our clothes. Though we change our clothes, the one who wears the clothes remains the same person. And similarly, though we have changed our physical body many times, the continuity of our mental consciousness remains, as it always has. Because we have had infinite previous lives, every sentient being, at one time or another, has been our parents, our very dear father, mother, relatives, friends, and so on. Every time that they were our very dear relatives and parents, they gave us so much love, so much care. They shielded us from many dangers, saved us from many harms, and gave us so many things and so much love. But today, we do not recognize each other in our present lives. We see only some as friends and relatives. Some we see as enemies, and toward others we are indifferent. But, in reality, every sentient being is our very dear previous mother, father, and so on. For these precious beings who have cared for us since beginningless times, we must develop compassion.

But mere compassion is not enough to rescue these sentient beings from the suffering of samsara. At the moment, we are ordinary people—we do not have sufficient wisdom, we do not have complete compassion, and we therefore do not have the power to rescue them. Also, we have no choice. Wherever the winds of karma blow, there we have to go as well. We can't choose where we will be born in our next life. We can't choose anything, so dependent are we on our own karma. This is why a person who is completely bound by karma and the defilements cannot liberate other sentient beings. Even the most powerful worldly deities with immense good qualities and immense miraculous abilities cannot rescue all sentient beings. Who can rescue them? Only fully enlightened buddhas who have removed all forms of obscuration and who possess every possible good quality can rescue sentient beings from samsara.

We claim to be followers of the Mahayana, the Great Vehicle. As Mahayana followers, our main goal, our sole purpose, is to accomplish full enlightenment for the sake of all sentient beings. It is for that purpose that we should receive these teachings. When we have that highest goal, then all other good qualities, such as overcoming obstacles in this life and gaining longevity, good health, prosperity, fulfillment of wishes, and so on, are naturally accomplished. When the main aim is the highest one, all good things are accomplished as a matter of course. For example, if a crop in general is good, then the grass, and the husk, and so on are naturally good as well.

Therefore, when receiving teachings, it is very important first to check your motivation. Question yourself and say, "Why am I receiving these teachings?" If the answer is for other purposes, it is not suitable. Try to create the right motivation. The best motivation is the aspiration to attain full enlightenment for the benefit of all sentient beings.

Now, we can't accomplish enlightenment without proper causes and conditions. In order to accomplish enlightenment we need to receive teachings. First we have to learn the teachings, and then after learning the teachings, we need to practice them in daily life. With such motivation, and with the body in a respectful posture, the voice in silence, and the mind concentrating on each and every word, we should receive the teachings.

COMPASSION IS THE ROOT

This particular teaching is called *Matchless Compassion Yoga*. Here, *yoga* refers to meditation.

Compassion is very, very important. It is the root of the Mahayana teachings, the Mahayana path, the Mahayana Dharma. If we lack compassion, whatever practice we do, whether generosity, moral conduct, patience, diligence, meditation, or even the very highest tantric practice, it does not become Mahayana Dharma. We may say it is Mahayana, or Vajrayana Dharma, but in reality it is not. It is Hinayana, or Lesser Vehicle, Dharma. Therefore, it is very, very important to make sure that first we develop compassion. Without compassion, the other qualities of buddhahood will not arise.

The great sixth-century Indian master Chandrakirti wrote *Engaging in the Middle Way*, a very important text that explains the view of ultimate truth distilled in the philosophy of the Madhyamaka, or Middle Way, school. When Chandrakirti wrote the book, he first paid homage to compassion. He didn't pay homage to the Buddha or to the bodhisattvas or to other deities. He paid homage to compassion because, as he explained, shravakas and pratyekabuddhas are born from the Buddha: the Buddha gave the teachings, they practiced them, and on the basis of that, they gained nirvana. Thus, without the Buddha, they could not have gained nirvana. Now, from whence is a buddha born? A buddha is born from a bodhisattva. A person first becomes a bodhisattva and then progresses on the bodhisattva path to accomplish full enlightenment. Without bodhisattvas, there are no buddhas. Now, from whence do bodhisattvas come? Bodhisattvas come from compassion, nondual thought, and enlightenment mind. It is from these causes that a bodhisattva is created. Thus the very root is compassion. The very first or original root of the great qualities of the buddhas and bodhisattvas lies in compassion.

When we fill a container with water, many drops of water are poured. The first drop, then the second drop, the third drop, and the accumulation of many drops eventually fill the container. Similarly, the very first root, the origin of the great qualities of the buddhas and bodhisattvas, is compassion. For us ordinary people, compassion is the very first seed or root of enlightenment within our minds. Therefore, compassion is crucially important.

Normally, we speak of loving kindness, compassion, and enlightenment mind, or *bodhichitta*. Loving kindness is like the love of every mother for her child. She wants her child to be physically healthy, mentally happy, and all of the wishes of that particular child to be fulfilled. Such kindly thoughts are termed *loving kindness*. Just as every parent loves his or her child, all of us have a certain amount of loving kindness. Not just we humans, but even fierce animals have a certain amount of loving kindness. However, at the moment, our loving kindness is very limited, in that it is based on selfish reasons. Our kind and loving thoughts typically arise because the object of our affection is a relative or a friend, and the like. Such loving kindness is not complete.

The loving kindness described in this teaching embraces every sentient being without discrimination, not distinguishing between those who are dearest to us and our most hated enemies. Such loving kindness is felt toward every sentient being without exception. Called *universal loving kindness*, it is very, very important. We must try to generate this loving kindness toward all sentient beings.

Next is compassion. There are many different levels of compassion. In general, compassion means to focus on a sentient being who is suffering—either physically or mentally—and have the wish for that being to be freed from his or her pain, freed from that suffering. This is called *compassion*. Of course we all have a certain amount of compassion. Whenever we see someone suffering, we all have some kind of feeling that wishes that particular being to be free of that suffering. But we do not have universal compassion, compassion toward all sentient beings. Ordinary beings lack this.

COMPASSION FOR OUR ENEMIES

The special technique of this particular text is to practice compassion toward a difficult object, because when we can practice compassion toward the most difficult object, it will be easy to develop compassion toward all other sentient beings. An example of a difficult object is an enemy, someone who seeks to harm us. It is very difficult to give rise to loving kindness and compassion for our enemies.

To do this, find a secluded place where there are no external disturbances or internal disturbances. It should be outwardly as well as inwardly completely peaceful. Your physical behavior should be completely balanced in the sense that you are not strenuously active and that you can completely relax. First take refuge in the Buddha, Dharma, and Sangha. This is vital. Then generate enlightenment mind. That is, think that for the benefit of all sentient beings, you must attain full enlightenment, and in order to attain enlightenment you are performing this practice. By taking refuge in the Triple Gem, you switch from the wrong path to the right path. By generating enlightenment mind, you move from the lower path to the higher Mahayana path.

Then visualize yourself in the form of any of the deities that you normally practice, such as Avalokiteshvara, Manjushri, or Vajrapani. To be able to carry out your practice successfully, without obstacles, and also to receive blessings, visualize your root guru on the top of your head. For example, if you are visualizing yourself in the form of Avalokiteshvara, then the guru should be in the form of Buddha Amitabha, who is master of Avalokiteshvara's buddha family or race. In other words, Avalokiteshvara's guru is Buddha Amitabha, so if you are visualizing yourself in the form of Avalokiteshvara, then visualize your own root guru in the form of Buddha Amitabha on the top of your head.

Now I will explain the actual practice. Visualize in front of you the most hated enemy that you can think of, the being you see as having harmed you the most. Try to practice compassion toward this enemy. Try to develop a genuine feeling of compassion for your enemy. Wish that this particular enemy will be happy and will be free from suffering and the causes of suffering. As you continue to practice this compassion, it is also important to alternate with contemplation of the reasons you should have compassion for your worst enemy. Practice the two in tandem: practice compassion and also the reason why you should develop compassion for your worst enemy.

So, with full concentration and with a single-pointed mind, very diligently focus on your most hated enemy, who is causing you a lot of damage, pain, and misery. Practice compassion toward this enemy. With this feeling, recite, "Toward this very harmful enemy, may I develop sympathy and feelings of compassion." Recite this many, many times until you have a real feeling of compassion.

Next is the reason why you have to develop compassion toward your worst enemy, and that contemplation proceeds as follows.

Our individual mind has existed from beginningless time. There is no moment of time that is the beginning of a particular person's mental consciousness. The mental consciousness cannot appear out of nowhere, and it cannot appear from a completely different thing like the elements, or from our present physical bodies, because the two are very different.

Just as rice will not grow from wheat, wheat will not grow from rice. To grow rice we need a rice seed, and to grow wheat we need a wheat seed. Similarly our mental consciousness cannot arise from mere elements, because the elements, like the physical body, are things that we can see and feel. We can describe their particular shape and particular colors. The mental consciousness is very different. It is something you can't touch and can't describe as having a particular shape or color.

Therefore, the mental consciousness must have arisen from a continuity of the same type as itself. One of the wonders of life is that it has no beginning; it has existed since beginningless time. Samsara has no beginning. From beginningless time until now we have been in samsara. It is impossible to describe the number of years, the number of eons, or the number of lives that we have experienced. Throughout countless lifetimes, countless eons, and countless periods of time we have been in samsara.

We have taken many different forms: human forms, animal forms, god forms, hungry ghost forms, and hell realm forms. And of course, every time we have taken a physical body, we have had parents, because we need parents to have a physical body. Thus, at one time or another, all sentient beings have actually been our very dear parents—our very dear mother, our very dear father—our very dear relatives, and our very dear friends. So in reality, this hated enemy is actually our own previous dear mother.

But, since we have changed lives, we do not recognize her. We see her as an enemy because we did not pay back the kindness and benefit that that mother gave us. We still carry an enormous debt and must repay her for her kindness and benefit. Now our very dear mother, our very dear father, our very dear relatives, and so on have appeared in the form of enemies requesting repayment of those debts. If we do not practice compassion, if we still look upon them as enemies and try to harm them, the result will be continuous suffering for ourselves and continuous suffering for others. When the hatred of both sides clashes, of course the result is deeply harmful.

Now, while we are free from all unfavorable conditions and while we have all necessary favorable conditions, it is vital that we take advantage of this golden opportunity. The best way to use this opportunity is to conquer our defilements—to conquer our hatred, to conquer our desire, and to conquer our ignorance. A person who can conquer the defilements is truly brave and can be called a real hero. For whether our mental hatred toward our enemies harms others or not, it will definitely send us to the lowest hell realms, where we will have to experience unimaginable and enormous suffering. No external enemy can do as much damage as our own internal mental hatred can. Therefore, this time, instead of destroying the outside enemy, we must destroy our worst enemy, our own hatred, through the practice of compassion. With the weapon of compassion, any defilement, any hatred, can be destroyed.

Contemplate the reasons why we ought to develop compassion toward our worst enemy. In reality this most hated enemy is also our own very dear mother or our very dear father. This is the first reason that instead of hatred, we must develop genuine compassion toward our enemy.

The second reason is that not only is our most hated enemy our very dear mother, he or she has been our mother not just once but for many, many lifetimes. Every time this enemy has been our mother, she has given us so much love, so much care, so much protection, and saved us from so much danger. For this reason too, we need to practice compassion.

The third reason is that every time this enemy has been our mother, he or she has given us so much benefit, as much benefit as our present mother gave us. In the beginning, our present mother gave us this precious body, this precious life. Without our mother, we wouldn't have life; without our mother, we wouldn't have this body; without our mother, we would not have survived; without our mother, we wouldn't have become a grown-up human being; without our mother, we would not have had the opportunity to practice Dharma. When we were first born, we were just like a tiny worm that could do nothing. But our mother did not let us die and took so much care of us and gave us so much benefit. Thus it is said that the first guru of our life was our own mother. Likewise, our enemy has done the same things and benefited us so much. That is why we need to practice compassion.

In summary, we need to develop compassion toward our most hated enemy because (1) that enemy is in reality our own mother, (2) that enemy was our mother not only once, but in many lifetimes, and (3) every time that enemy was our mother, she gave us so much benefit, so much love, and so much kindness. For these reasons we need to develop genuine loving kindness and compassion toward our enemy.

Next is the fourth reason. Although this greatly hated enemy is your own mother, at the moment, instead of benefitting you, he or she is causing you great harm. Why? The reason is that your past mother is mentally disturbed—she is being controlled by hatred—and lacking self-control, she performs all kinds of harmful actions. Your most hated enemy is in reality your own mother, but in the circumstances of the new life, he or she is possessed by hatred like a lunatic and has no choice and no freedom to stop causing you pain.

Say your own mother, father, relative, or whoever is dearest to you in this life were to become mentally deranged and do a lot of damage to you—hitting you, injuring you, or whatever. You would not feel hatred, for you would realize that this person has no choice. No matter what mentally disturbed people do, we do not get angry because we know that person has no choice. In the same way, our enemies have no choice when completely under the control of hatred. They have become like lunatics or mentally disturbed people. Without being able to choose otherwise, they cause great harm to others, even to us, their own children. This is the fourth reason that we must develop compassion instead of hatred: our enemy is completely possessed by hatred and has no choice but to harm us.

Another reason we should develop compassion is that as a result of constantly indulging in hatred and causing harm to us, our enemy will be reborn in the hell realms, such as the worst hell realm known as Avici, where there is enormous, unimaginable suffering. Therefore, we must develop compassion toward those who have hatred, because their indulgence in hatred will bring them immense suffering. Realize that in return for such hatred, all they will get is immense suffering. Thus this enemy who constantly indulges in hatred and causes great harm to others will suffer unimaginably in the lowest realms. This is another reason why we must develop genuine compassion toward our enemies.

In this way, contemplate your enemies and count the reasons to develop compassion toward them; concentrate on the causes of compassion. Practice compassion in this way until you have a real inner feeling, such that tears fall from your eyes or the hairs on your body stand up. Try to practice until you have such genuine feelings of compassion.

When instead of hatred we have developed such genuine feelings of compassion toward our worst enemy, who causes us great harm, then extend these feelings toward all beings and develop enlightenment mind. Think that for the sake of all sentient beings, and especially for the sake of our most hated enemy, we must attain enlightenment. In order to save all sentient beings, and especially to save our hated enemy from the suffering of samsara, we must attain buddhahood. May this harmful enemy and all sentient beings also be able to accomplish buddhahood. With such thoughts, try to meditate on primordial wisdom free of elaboration.

Some other teachings begin by developing compassion toward an easy object, such as relatives or family, and then move to enemies, and eventually to all sentient beings. But this particular teaching does it in the opposite order, beginning with the most difficult object—our enemies. This is because, having developed genuine compassion toward the most difficult object, it is easy for it to arise toward other objects. Once you have compassion instead of hatred for your enemy, it is easy for compassion to arise for beings toward whom you are indifferent and toward your neighbors, fellow countrymen, relatives, and so on. The goal is to eventually develop compassion toward all sentient beings, with no exceptions, and to have the same amount of compassion for every single sentient being.

This meditation on compassion has great benefits. It eliminates anger and hatred, which cause many physical pains. When your mind experiences hatred and defilements, the tension and stress causes various physical illnesses and a lot of damage to the body. When you eliminate hatred, many physical pains and illnesses also disappear.

This meditation also develops genuine compassion toward all sentient beings as if they were your only child. Of course every mother loves her children, but mothers who have only one child have a very special kind of loving kindness and compassion toward that child. Practice compassion and think about the benefits of practicing compassion until you develop such a feeling.

Think about the consequences you will face if you do not develop compassion. If you continue to indulge in hatred, what will you face? As Shantideva said, "All the virtuous deeds of generosity, making offerings, and so on"—keeping vows, doing meditation, or recitation of prayers—"that we have accumulated over thousands of eons can be ruined by one moment of hatred." Thus, there is no greater nonvirtue than the arising of hatred; it is the most harmful action we can perform.

The minute hatred or anger arises in the mind, you are no longer peaceful. Peace and harmony are completely destroyed. If someone possesses anger or hatred, wherever they go, the peace and harmony of the area will be destroyed. All conflicts, all disturbances, all terrors, and all miseries in this world are caused by hatred. There is no action worse than indulging in hatred. Therefore, try to dispel hatred by every possible means.

RELATIVE ENLIGHTENMENT MIND: EXCHANGING SELF FOR OTHERS

After genuine compassion is developed, then we develop enlightenment mind. The main cause of accomplishing buddhahood is enlightenment mind, or *bodhichitta*. Enlightenment mind is of two kinds: relative and absolute. Relative, or conventional, enlightenment mind is the wish to become enlightened in order to save all beings from cyclic existence. Absolute, or ultimate, enlightenment mind is the nonconceptual primordial wisdom free of elaboration. It can only be attained through concentration and meditation.

There are many different methods for cultivating relative enlightenment mind. The most important of these is exchange meditation. *Exchange meditation* means to give all your benefit, all your happiness, all your peace to other sentient beings and to take upon yourself all other sentient beings' pain, misery, and sufferings. This is exchange meditation, or exchange of self and others.

Your best opportunity to do this meditation is when you are sick, when you have great sorrow or mental suffering, physical pain, or great fear, or when you outwardly have disturbances in the elements or inwardly have great defilements. Instead of indulging in a negative way in response to such circumstances, use them as an opportunity for exchange meditation. For example, if you are feeling anger or hatred toward others, then do this meditation to avoid harming other beings.

Normally if we don't like someone and think of the harm that they have caused, hatred arises. We want that particular person to die, to have harm befall them, and so on. Having such thoughts again and again leads to taking physical action, such as killing the person or otherwise injuring them. Verbally you may say unkind words, very harsh words, which cause pain in that person's mind. Mentally of course, you have great anger and great hatred, which brings pain and suffering for yourself and leads to further negative actions.

Now when such hatred for someone arises, instead of following it, imagine taking all other sentient beings' hatred into you, so that it ripens upon your self and so that all other sentient beings may be thereby freed from such harmful hatred.

There is another method. Sentient beings have many defilements, or mental disturbances, which are causes, and the result of indulging in such defilements is great physical and mental suffering. Of course, the root of all of this suffering is self-clinging—believing in the reality of a solid, permanent self that must be defended. This self-clinging is the root defilement from which all suffering springs. For this method, think, "May all of the sufferings of other sentient beings—all of their physical pain, mental anxieties, shortcomings, and everything—fall upon me. And may all of my positive karma and happiness be given to all other sentient beings." Doing this crushes our self-clinging, and when our self-clinging is crushed, of course we become free of suffering. So instead of saying, "Protect me! Save me! May I be free from this suffering! May I enjoy happiness!" and so on, think, "May all suffering, all harm, all damage, all misery be thrown upon me." This crushes self-clinging, and by doing it, you are able to overcome all suffering.

The reason is this: The buddhas and bodhisattvas devote their full life and energy for others' benefit, and as a result, they accomplish their own purpose, in the sense that they are totally free from suffering. They also accomplish the purposes of others because they can provide immense benefit to other sentient beings. Ordinary sentient beings, since beginningless time, have cared only for themselves, clinging only to themselves. The result is more and more suffering, and more and more harm to themselves and others. Realizing this, practice compassion, first toward loved ones, then toward enemies, and eventually toward all beings in every different realm.

For example, in the hell realms there is immense and unimaginable suffering from cold, heat, torture, and misery. Among hungry ghosts, there is so much suffering from hunger and thirst for very long periods of time, hundreds and thousands of years. We can see how animals suffer, how they are tortured, forced to work, and slaughtered. Animals, of course, kill each other, too. Powerful animals like lions and tigers kill countless other beings. Human beings also do a lot of damage to them. These are the sufferings of animals.

In the higher realms, demigods also suffer. They are said to be constantly engaged in battle with the gods, but since their merit is never equal to that of the gods, they are always defeated, and so they also suffer immensely. And although gods have a very luxurious life that is full of pleasures, it is not permanent, and one day it ends. As their lives end, they see that they will fall down into the lower realms, where they must endure unimaginable physical suffering. When they realize this, they have tremendous mental suffering. We human beings also have so much suffering. Generally speaking, we are not free from the four major sufferings, the sufferings of birth, aging, sickness, and death. There are also the special sufferings of those who are terminally ill, impoverished, without food and clothing, or severely handicapped.

So think, "May all of these sufferings of samsara ripen upon me; may all obstacles and unfavorable conditions of the path ripen upon me." In this way, you take every sentient being's suffering and misery upon yourself.

As you do the meditation, recite aloud, "May all sentient beings' sufferings ripen upon me." Visualize that your own benefit, your own merit, your own wisdom, your own virtuous deeds, and your own happiness all radiate out like sunshine and are given to sentient beings. As they receive these benefits, think that all sentient beings become physically healthy and mentally happy. Eventually they come to possess all of the qualities of the path and ultimately accomplish buddhahood. Also recite, "By my virtuous deeds, may all sentient beings accomplish happiness."

Practicing relative enlightenment mind in this way temporarily dispels all thoughts and defilements and also overcomes all sicknesses and obstacles. It will have immense benefit and impact on other beings too. Eventually you will be able to accomplish buddhahood, which is the dharmakaya, sambhogakaya, and nirmanakaya, through which you will be able to benefit all sentient beings.

ABSOLUTE ENLIGHTENMENT MIND

The method for developing absolute enlightenment mind is through meditation. First do concentration meditation (*shamatha*) until the mind is able to remain single pointedly in complete calmness. Then on the basis of this, meditate on insight wisdom (*vipashyana*). The stability of calm-abiding meditation and the wisdom of insight meditation merge together, and through this it becomes possible to accomplish the dharmakaya. Then your own awareness, which is the primordial wisdom of a single moment, becomes buddhahood. Non-conceptual primordial wisdom is the dharmakaya, self-awareness is the sambhogakaya, and clarity is the nirmanakaya. The inseparability of these three different aspects is the svabhavakaya.

We all possess buddha nature in the sense that the true nature of our minds is away from all activity. To say that the true nature of mind is away from all activity means that it is completely removed from descriptions such as "existence," "nonexistence," "both," "neither," and so on. It is fully imbued with the five enlightened wisdoms. This consciousness, the true nature of the mind, which is removed from all activity, is the wisdom of the dharmadhatu, or ultimate reality. The wisdom that is realized is mirror-like wisdom, self-awareness is the wisdom of discrimination, clarity is the wisdom of accomplishment, and the indivisibility of all of these different aspects is the wisdom of equality.

This preliminary practice was given by Mahasiddha Virupa. Maha siddha Virupa had innumerable disciples when he was the abbot of Nalanda Monastery, thousands and thousands of monks and other students. After he left the monastery and became a mahasiddha, he also had many, many disciples. Through his performance of extraordinary physical, verbal, and mental activities, he benefitted an immense number of sentient beings, all of whom are counted as his disciples. However, as far as lineage holders are concerned, he had two main disciples.

One was Krishnapa, who was his main disciple in the Lamdre tradition. As we saw in Virupa's life story, Krishnapa had been a non-Buddhist yogi and not a Buddhist at all, but after seeing Mahasiddha

Virupa's great qualities, he followed Virupa and became his disciple. Virupa taught him by the gradual path. The gradual path is actually called the *less fortunate path*, because it does not allow you to enter the Vajrayana path directly. To enter the Vajrayana path, you must first enter the Hinayana path, then proceed to the Mahayana, then the lower tantras, eventually reaching the highest tantra. The disciple Krishnapa was an example of a disciple who needed to be led by the gradual path.

Virupa's other main disciple was Dombi Heruka, or Dombipa. He was led by the direct path. The direct path, the *fortunate path*, allows you to enter the Vajrayana path directly without first proceeding through the other paths. Mahasiddha Virupa gave this teaching to Dombi Heruka, and eventually it came to Tibet.

On whichever path you follow—the Mahayana path, and especially the Vajrayana path, which includes visualizations, recitations, and foundation practices—all practices are of course very, very important. But the most important practice of all is the cultivation of compassion. Without compassion, no matter what you do, it will not be the direct cause of enlightenment. For a practice to be a direct cause of enlightenment, you must have enlightenment mind. And to have proper enlightenment mind, you need compassion. Without compassion you can't have the other qualities.

It is said that Avalokiteshvara was once asked by a disciple, "What practice is the most essential to accomplish buddhahood?" Avalokiteshvara answered that the most important thing, the most essential thing to do to attain buddhahood, is to practice compassion. This is because when you practice compassion, all other qualities, such as loving kindness and the enlightenment mind, are naturally accomplished and naturally gather. When you invite the emperor, you do not need to invite each and every member of his entourage. Wherever the emperor goes, his entourage will follow. Similarly, whoever practices compassion will find that other qualities are naturally accomplished.

Therefore, compassion is the most important thing in the beginning, in the middle, and after accomplishing the result. Throughout the path, at all times, compassion is the most important thing. Therefore, everyday, in every practice, we must try to develop compassion.

With this we have completed the teaching.

PART THREE

Parting from the Four Attachments

Sachen Kunga Nyingpo (1092–1158) surrounded by the other four of the five founders of the Sakya order, clockwise from top left: Sonam Tsemo, Dragpa Gyaltsen, Chogyal Phagpa, and Sakya Pandita

Parting from the Four Attachments *is a renowned mind-training teaching that was received directly from Manjushri, the bodhisattva of wisdom, by the first of the five founders of our order, Sachen Kunga Nyingpo, when he was only twelve years old. A mere four lines long, it is a great classic summary of the entire Mahayana path. Included in this section is an extensive explanation of this teaching that I gave in 2003. This was the first teaching that I bestowed at Tsechen Kunchab Ling in Walden, New York, my temple seat in the United States. This commentary is based on the fifteenth-century commentary by Ngorchen Kunga Zangpo.*

Study of this section should proceed in the following order: study, contemplation, and then meditation. For study, four commentaries by some of the Sakya order's most famous founders and scholars are included here. The commentaries are presented in historical order, beginning with the earliest masters.

Study this great teaching again and again at gradually deeper levels of explanation. Contemplate it carefully, and eventually the true meaning and relationships between the concepts in the teachings will arise. Meditate on these teachings starting with the preliminary prayers explained in the commentaries, and then according to the explanations, and if questions arise, try to consult a qualified teacher. At the end of the meditation session, conclude with the dedication prayer at the end of the book.

You will find great continuity among the commentaries. This continuity is considered a mark of excellent Buddhist scholarship, for it is through such continuity with the sutras themselves and with the teachings of earlier masters that the authentic path of the Buddha has been preserved for over 2,500 years. From these commentaries, new students of Buddhism can understand how carefully and authentically succeeding generations of great scholars and practitioners have studied, meditated, realized, and taught the central truths of the Buddha's teachings.

—

The Life Story of Sachen Kunga Nyingpo

SAKYAPA NGAWANG KUNGA SONAM (1597–1659)

SACHEN KUNGA NYINGPO was the first of the five great masters who founded the Sakya order of Tibetan Buddhism. He was born in Sakya, Tibet, in the year 1092. His father was Khon Konchog Gyalpo, who established Sakya Monastery in 1073. His mother was Machig Zhangmo.

Sachen Kunga Nyingpo was an emanation of Avalokiteshvara. Many auspicious signs occurred at the time of his birth. Because all who saw him were filled with joy, he was named Kunga Nyingpo, which means "essence of joy for all."

Sachen Kunga Nyingpo was blessed with exceptional intelligence, and while very young he studied reading, mathematics, astrology, and elegant discourse. He also thoroughly studied and mastered aesthetics, medicine, Sanskrit, poetry, composition, and other subjects, and became a recognized master of all of these fields. From his father he received the Hevajra empowerment and many other Dharma teachings.

When Sachen Kunga Nyingpo was eleven years old, his father, Khon Konchog Gyalpo, passed away. Sachen Kunga Nyingpo was still too young to hold the responsibility of the monastery, so his mother Machig Zhangmo appointed the great translator Bari Lotsawa as abbot of Sakya Monastery until Sachen Kunga Nyingpo became an adult. On the same day, Machig Zhangmo also arranged for the laying of the foundation stones for a new shrine and performance of the funeral rites for Khon Konchog Gyalpo.

That year, Bari Lotsawa recommended that Sachen Kunga Nyingpo perform an extended retreat on Manjushri, the bodhisattva of wisdom. Even though he was only eleven years old, as a future throne holder, he would need to develop great wisdom. At the beginning of the retreat, various obstacles arose that were overcome by the practice of the deity Achala. Gradually all hindrances were pacified, and Sachen Kunga Nyingpo developed great meditative realization.

After six months of meditation, Sachen Kunga Nyingpo perceived Manjushri himself in his retreat cabin. Manjushri bestowed upon him a four-line verse that Sachen Kunga Nyingpo immediately realized to be a summary of the entire Mahayana path to enlightenment. This profound teaching became known as *Parting from the Four Attachments*.

At the same time, Manjushri blessed Sachen Kunga Nyingpo with a prophetic vision. Seven wisdom swords emanated from Manjushri's heart and were absorbed into Sachen Kunga Nyingpo's heart, symbolizing that seven successive emanations of Manjushri would appear among Sachen Kunga Nyingpo's descendants and that his lineage would be forever blessed by this wisdom deity. Through the blessing of this vision, Sachen Kunga Nyingpo developed great wisdom and became able to effortlessly understand all phenomena.

Sachen Kunga Nyingpo continued his extensive training. When he was twelve years old, his teachers decided that he should go to study Abhidharma philosophy at Rong Ngurmig with Drangti Darma Nyingpo, who was the most famous teacher of the subject at that time. When Sachen Kunga Nyingpo arrived at Drangti's monastery, there was no space for him in the monks' quarters because of the many students already studying there. Sachen Kunga Nyingpo made himself a simple shelter from a curtain and stayed in the courtyard. Another monk staying nearby contracted smallpox and was very ill with no one to nurse him. Moved by great compassion, Sachen Kunga Nyingpo nursed him until he recovered, as a result of which he contracted smallpox himself. Sachen Kunga Nyingpo became severely ill. His mother visited to comfort and encourage him, and gradually he recovered.

Finally he received the *Treasury of the Abhidharma* by Vasubandu teaching once from Drangti Darma Nyingpo. After only one hearing, he completely memorized the words and fully understood the meaning. Everyone was amazed at his ability. After that, Sachen Kunga Nyingpo began the study of logic.

At this point, the leaders of Sakya Monastery encouraged Sachen Kunga Nyingpo to temporarily set aside the study of logic and to return to Sakya Monastery to receive teachings and transmissions from the great translator Bari Lotsawa, who had become very advanced in years. Bari Lotsawa gave him many teachings on the sutras, including commentaries on the Perfection of Wisdom sutras, the Heap of Jewels (Ratnakuta) sutras, and others. Bari Lotsawa also gave him many important teachings from the tantras, including about two hundred sections of action tantra, Yamantaka and Mahakrodha Vijaya from the performance tantras, the *Root Guhyasamaja Tantra* and its associated explanatory texts from the highest yoga tantras, tantric commentaries written by Nagarjuna, and many other teachings.

Bari Lotsawa presented Sachen Kunga Nyingpo with a stone statue of the deity Mahakala known as the Wish-Fulfilling Jewel. This holy statue is one of the four streams by which the Mahakala teachings converged in the Sakya tradition. Bari Lotsawa transferred the throne of the Sakya Monastery to Sachen Kunga Nyingpo and not long afterward passed away.

Sachen Kunga Nyingpo continued to receive many teachings and empowerments from other renowned teachers. Although he had previously received teachings on the three Hevajra tantras from his father, he also received an extensive version of these teachings from Khon Gyichuwa Dralabar, as well as additional commentaries, supplementary teachings, detailed pith instructions, and others. Each of these teachings he swiftly mastered. Sachen Kunga Nyingpo was the most intelligent among Khon Gyichuwa Dralabar's eighty disciples and understood the meaning of all of the texts.

Khon Gyichuwa Dralabar passed away, and in his will, he appointed Sachen Kunga Nyingpo as leader of his disciples and monastery, a position that Sachen Kunga Nyingpo accepted. He considered taking monastic ordination, but one of his other teachers recommended that if he remained a lay person, it would be of far greater benefit to Lord Buddha's doctrine and sentient beings.

Sachen Kunga Nyingpo visited the great translator Mal Lotsawa and received many teachings from him on a wide variety of tantras, including especially the *Chakrasamvara* root and explanation tantras. Some years later Mal Lotsawa invited Sachen Kunga Nyingpo to visit again and gave him extensive additional initiations and teachings, including particularly the Mahakala empowerment and meditation practice.

Mal Lotsawa gave Sachen Kunga Nyingpo a black flag that was a holy object of Mahakala, a steel vajra with nine prongs, and the Mahakala mask known as Senbag Nagpo Phurzhi. This mask is particularly sacred and is the most excellent among the four converging streams of Mahakala in the shrine in Sakya. When he bestowed these holy objects upon Sachen Kunga Nyingpo, Mal Lotsawa spoke to Mahakala as one person might speak to another, saying, "Now I am so old I don't need you. From now on follow the Khon Sakyapa and their descendants and do whatever they instruct."

Desiring to receive the precious Lamdre teaching, Sachen Kunga Nyingpo searched for the great Lama Shangton Chobar and finally found him at Sagthang. For the next eight years, he received the Lamdre teaching in a very detailed manner and meditated upon it carefully. Finally, when the oral instructions were completed, Lama Shangton Chobar gave these instructions to Sachen Kunga Nyingpo:

"For the next eighteen years, do not allow even the name of this teaching to pass your lips. Needless to say, do not teach or transmit it to others nor set it down in writing. After eighteen years, you will become the owner of this teaching, and at that time, if you wish to write it down or teach it to others, the decision is entirely yours." Saying thus, he completely concealed the teachings.

Lama Shangton Chobar also prophesized to Sachen Kunga Nyingpo, "If you concentrate primarily on practice, you will reach the excellent attainment of great mahamudra within this life. However, if you concentrate primarily on teaching the Dharma to others, it will benefit countless beings. In particular, three of your disciples will reach the excellent attainment of great mahamudra without abandoning their bodies. Seven of your disciples will reach the stage of patience, and about eighty will attain high realization."

So as to be sure not to forget the precious Lamdre teaching, Sachen Kunga Nyingpo made the commitment to contemplate it in its entirety once a month and to recite the *Vajra Verses* six or seven times each day. He strictly observed Lama Shangton Chobar's instructions not to mention or write down the teaching.

After eighteen years had passed, Lama Aseng learned that Sachen Kunga Nyingpo possessed the Lamdre teaching and came to him to request instruction. Sachen Kunga Nyingpo thought that this was an auspicious omen, and so he taught the Lamdre teaching to Lama Aseng alone. He also wrote the *Condensed Meaning of Lamdre (Lamdre Donduma)*.

After that, according to various disciples' requests, Sachen Kunga Nyingpo gave the Lamdre teaching many times and composed eleven commentaries on it. Among them, the Lamdre written for Geshe Nyag (the so-called *Nyagma*) was the most well written, with the fullest explication of the meaning and the most concise exposition. This text is the primary one used today.

Among Sachen Kunga Nyingpo's disciples, eleven heart disciples upheld the lineage of the Lamdre oral instructions, and seven heart disciples wrote commentaries on his writings. There were four well-known great masters who were accomplished in both learning and realization.

The great Sachen Kunga Nyingpo held the throne of the Sakya order for forty-eight years, from the age of twenty to sixty-seven. He brought the precious Lamdre teachings and Mahakala practice into the Sakya order and firmly established the Sakya tradition of great learning and meditation. As prophesized, he also bore sons who were emanations of Manjushri, among them Sonam Tsemo and Jetsun Dragpa Gyaltsen, who are counted as the second and third founders of the Sakya order.

In the year of the Male Earth Tiger (1158), at Yeru Kyawo Khadang, on the fourteenth day of the Tibetan month of Takar, Sachen Kunga Nyingpo departed peacefully for the next world, welcomed by a great assembly of viras and dakinis. At the time of his passing, even common people heard the sound of celestial music, smelled a heavenly aroma that pervaded the entire area, and saw the sky filled with light and rainbows. Most witnessed his body manifest four different aspects as it departed. One aspect departed for Sukhavati, another for the Potala pure realm, a third for Oddiyana, and the fourth aspect departed for the Copper-Colored Paradise in the north. After cremation, Sachen Kunga Nyingpo's holy ashes were deposited in a lake, and the mandala of Chakrasamvara appeared on the surface of the lake as clearly as if it had been painted.

Excerpted from *Sakya Dungrab Chenmo*. Translated by Khenpo Kalsang Gyaltsen and Ani Kunga Chodron.

Root Verses of
Parting from the Four Attachments

SACHEN KUNGA NYINGPO (1092–1158)

If you have attachment to this life, you are not a religious
person.

If you have attachment to the world of existence, you do not
have renunciation.

If you have attachment to your own purpose, you do not have
enlightenment mind.

If grasping arises, you do not have the view.

Explanation of
Parting from the Four Attachments

His Holiness Sakya Trizin

THIS TEACHING is from the category of teachings known as mind training (*lojong*). It was given directly by the great bodhisattva Manjushri to the great Lama Sakyapa, Sachen Kunga Nyingpo.

HOW TO RECEIVE THE TEACHINGS

When receiving teachings, first we develop right motivation. The teachings we receive and the practices we do will eventually produce a result according to our motivation. Therefore, it is very important to generate the right motivation.

The right motivation is to think that as space has no limits, so too the number of sentient beings is without limit. Although all of them long for happiness and wish to be free of suffering, yet overpowered by ignorance, the majority of them are experiencing suffering currently and are creating the causes of future suffering. Think that therefore our main goal is to rescue all these suffering sentient beings by attaining perfect enlightenment. The purpose of receiving this precious teaching is to attain enlightenment, and after receiving the teaching, we will very diligently follow the path. Developing this type of right motivation is very important.

Next, we practice right conduct. It is inappropriate to sit in a disrespectful posture—to lie down and the like. When receiving teachings, sit with the body in a respectful posture, with the voice in silence, and with the mind single-pointedly filled with great joy. We feel joy because it is very rare for buddhas to appear in this universe, and also it is very rare to obtain a precious human life, and even more rare to have the good fortune to receive such precious teachings. Today, all of these very rare conditions are gathered together, so we rejoice.

Freedom from the three faults of a container

It is also said that when receiving teachings, students should be free from the three faults of a container. The first fault is likened to an upside-down container. In this case, no matter what is poured, nothing enters. Similarly, students may be sitting before the teacher, but unless they are paying attention to the teaching, their minds are like upside-down containers.

The second fault occurs when the container is right-side up but has holes in it. In this case, whatever good things are poured in enter, but then they run right out again and do not remain. This happens when students may be listening to the teaching but not mindfully trying to retain what is said, so later they don't remember anything at all.

The third fault occurs when the container is right-side up and has no holes but has impure things inside it. Whatever good things are poured in mix with the impure things and are spoiled as a result. Likewise, receiving teachings with a mind filled with wrong motivation and negative emotions pollutes our understanding and brings little benefit. Thus students should strive to free their minds from wrong thoughts, wrong motivation, and negative emotions.

Avoiding the six wrong attitudes and cultivating the six right attitudes

Not only should we avoid the three faults of a contianer, we should also avoid the six wrong attitudes. The first is pride. For example, we may be proud of being born into a higher social class. While listening to the teachings, some may think, "I am from a higher class, or I am more learned than the teacher." When we listen to the teachings with a proud attitude, it is as in the saying, "On the mounds of pride, no water remains." Pride is like a mound on the ground that causes the water of beneficial instruction to run off and not sink in. Pride is the first wrong attitude.

The second wrong attitude is seeking faults in the master and the teachings instead of cultivating faith and devotion. This type of disrespect is also a very wrong attitude.

The third wrong attitude is a lack of real enthusiasm or faith in the teachings. Although a student may be listening, he or she may be motivated primarily by idle curiosity, without sincere interest in actually practicing the Dharma.

The fourth is to sit in the teachings while the mind is distracted by other external phenomena.

The fifth wrong attitude is distraction. This could mean to receive teachings while being distracted by conceptual thoughts of the past, present, and future. Another variant is to engage in meditation while attending a teaching. Students should follow the sequence of first receiving teachings, next contemplating them, and only then meditating. It is not appropriate to meditate during teachings; meditation should be done later. It is better to fill the mind with great joy and enthusiasm for the opportunity to hear the Dharma.

The sixth wrong attitude is despair, or fatigue. There are two types of despair: despair that the sessions are too long and despair that the profound meaning of the teachings is not easily understood. If despair arises, think that this is a rare and wonderful opportunity to receive the teachings and try to be patient even if the sessions are long. If you despair because you don't understand the teachings, remember that receiving the teaching several times is the best remedy for a lack of understanding. By receiving more teachings, you become better able to understand them.

Thus students should be free of the three faults of a container and the six wrong attitudes. In contrast, they should possess the six right attitudes, which are to see the spiritual master as a doctor, themselves as patients, the teaching as a very effective medicine, their defilements as a severe illness, and practice of the teachings as the therapy. The omniscient Buddha's method is flawless, and the result will surely be effective.

Receiving the teachings as practice of the six perfections

The act of receiving the teachings with a mind free of the three faults and six wrong attitudes and possessing the six right attitudes is in itself a great practice. Another explanation describes how listening to teachings can become a practice of the six bodhisattva perfections.

The first perfection, generosity, is practiced when the disciple offers the mandala and other things to the teacher and the teacher offers the Dharma teaching. The second perfection, moral conduct, is a disciple's abstention from wrong actions while listening to the teachings. Being physically, verbally, and mentally patient while receiving the teachings is the third perfection, patience. Greatly rejoicing in the teachings and taking great interest in them is the fourth perfection, diligence. Single-pointedly concentrating on the profound meaning of the teachings is the fifth perfection, meditation. The sixth perfection, wisdom, is gained through receiving the teachings and then contemplating and meditating on them.

In this way, properly receiving the teachings becomes in itself an excellent practice of the six perfections.

HISTORY OF THE TEACHING

Sachen Kunga Nyingpo, also known as Lama Sakyapa, was the first of the five great founders of the Sakya order. He is considered the lineage holder of four great translators, among whom Bari Lotsawa Rinchen Dragpa is one.

When the great Lama Sachen Kunga Nyingpo was twelve years old, his master, Bari Lotsawa, advised him, "Since you are the son of a great master, it is important that you study the scriptures. To study, you need to acquire wisdom, and in order to acquire wisdom, you need to practice Manjushri, the bodhisattva of wisdom." Saying thus, Bari Lotsawa bestowed the initiation of the saffron-colored Manjushri and the related teachings.

Soon after, the young Lama Sakyapa undertook a retreat on Manjushri under the guidance of Bari Lotsawa. In the beginning there were certain signs of obstacles, which were removed through the practice of the wrathful deity Achala. After six months of retreat, Manjushri appeared in Lama Sakyapa's pure vision amid offerings and rainbows and a shower of flowers. Manjushri was seated on a jeweled throne as if it were a chair, with two legs hanging down, attended by two bodhisattvas. At that time, Manjushri uttered this teaching of just four lines, saying:

> If you have attachment to this life, you are not a religious person.
> If you have attachment to the world of existence, you do not have renunciation.
> If you have attachment to your own purpose, you do not have enlightenment mind.
> If grasping arises, you do not have the view.

Analyzing this teaching, the young Lama Sakyapa realized that these four lines included the entire profound practice of the sutric path.

In reality the great Lama Sakyapa Kunga Nyingpo was himself an emanation of both Manjushri and Avalokiteshvara. He did not need to acquire additional wisdom. However, since he was born in a human body, he followed the general process of ordinary beings' lives by appearing to study and receive these teachings.

Lama Sakyapa gave this teaching to his sons and disciples, and they gave it to their sons and disciples, and thus it has been passed down to this day. I myself received this teaching from my main guru, Dampa Dorje Chang of Ngor Monastery. I also received this teaching from His Eminence Chogye Trichen Rinpoche.

At all Sakya monasteries, this is the preliminary teaching. Because it is a very authentic and profound pith instruction given directly by Manjushri, it is recognized as a profound teaching by all of the traditions of Tibetan Buddhism. It is included in many collections of mind-training teachings.

This type of teaching is known as a pith instruction. The Buddha gave innumerable teachings of many different types and levels. In general, these can be classified into two kinds: vast, general teachings, like sutras and commentaries, that are studied over a long period of time and slowly put into practice; and pith instructions for those who do not have time for vast and detailed study. Great masters who have accomplished high realization write pith instructions based on their own experience that provide a guide for practice in a nutshell, which disciples can put straight into practice.

PRELIMINARIES

This pith instruction has three sections: preliminaries, main part, and conclusion. Although the preliminaries are not explicitly mentioned in the four lines of the teaching, we always begin with the preliminaries. There are two parts to the preliminaries: taking refuge and creating enlightenment mind.

Taking refuge

The purpose of taking refuge is to change from the wrong path to the right path. Not performing any virtuous practice, or performing virtuous practice in the wrong way, is considered the wrong path. By changing from the wrong path to the right path, you enter the path of liberation and enlightenment. Although taking refuge in the Triple Gem is common to all the Buddhist traditions, the Mahayana practice of taking refuge has four special characteristics.

The first special characteristic is the *objects* in which you take refuge. All Buddhists take refuge in the Buddha, Dharma, and Sangha. However, in the Mahayana Buddhist tradition, the Buddha is defined as the matchless one who possesses limitless perfect qualities and is free from all faults. In the Mahayana tradition also, buddhas are said to possess the three bodies, or *kayas*: the dharmakaya, the sambhogakaya, and the nirmanakaya.

The dharmakaya is the "body of reality" that possesses double purity. The first purity is the buddha nature that every sentient being possesses. This buddha nature is the true nature of mind that is never stained by obscurations. Although ordinary beings possess this basic purity, it is not realized, as it is completely hidden by obscurations that prevent the real nature from being seen. Through the accumulation of merit and wisdom, buddhas purify all forms of obscurations. This is the second purity, which allows the original, real nature of the mind to be seen.

The second of the three bodies of a buddha is the sambhogakaya, the "body of enjoyment." Not only through the accumulation of wisdom, but also through the accumulation of great merit, all the obscurations are purified, and enormous good qualities of body, voice, and mind are attained. These magnificent physical qualities characterize the sambhogakaya.

The sambhogakaya possesses five certainties. This holy body is beyond birth and death and is adorned with the perfect major and minor marks; it always remains in the highest buddha realm, it gives only Mahayana teachings, its disciples are only the highest bodhisattvas, and it constantly turns the wheel of Dharma until the end of samsara.

The third of the bodies of a buddha is the nirmanakaya, the "body of emanations." In this body, the buddha appears out of great compassion, wherever, whenever, and in whatever form is required to help the sentient beings. The historical Shakyamuni Buddha was a nirmanakaya, as even ordinary beings could see his physical body and receive teachings.

Possession of these three bodies is a characteristic of buddhas, our peerless guides.

The second object in which we take refuge is the Dharma, which is the Buddha's precious teaching. The word *dharma* actually has many different meanings in different contexts. As an object of refuge, the holy Dharma has two aspects. The first aspect is the Mahayana scriptures such as the sutras, the tantras, and the vinaya. The second aspect is the realization accomplished by the buddhas and bodhisattvas.

The third object of refuge is the Sangha, or the holy community. In the Mahayana tradition this means the bodhisattvas who have already reached the irreversible stage and practice in accordance with right behavior and understanding; they are the true Sangha.

The second special characteristic of Mahayana refuge is the *duration* of refuge. Mahayana refuge is not just for a certain period of time until a temporary goal is reached, or even just until the end of this lifetime. We take refuge from the moment that we receive the vow until we reach our ultimate goal of becoming a perfect and fully enlightened Buddha.

The third special characteristic of Mahayana refuge is the *person* who takes refuge. We imagine not just ourselves alone, but all sentient beings taking refuge. There are three causes of taking refuge: *fear* of the suffering of samsara, *faith* in the good qualities of the Triple Gem, and *compassion* for sentient beings. With compassion, we realize that although all sentient beings were our very dear ones in previous lives, we no longer recognize them in this new life. Therefore, we take refuge not only for ourselves, but for all sentient beings.

The fourth special characteristic of Mahayana refuge is the *purpose* of taking refuge. We take refuge not just to save ourselves alone but to save countless sentient beings as infinite as space. If you look with compassion at the situation of beings in the universe of samsara, you can see that all of them are currently in the midst of suffering and are creating even more causes of suffering. A feeling of great compassion and concern for their condition arises. To rescue them, you need to take refuge.

Although all three causes of taking refuge—fear, faith, and compassion—may be present in your mind, in the Mahayana tradition, the main cause is compassion.

Keeping these things in mind, recite the actual refuge prayer:

> I and all other sentient beings equalling the limits of space
>   who have previously been my mothers,
> from this time until the essence of enlightenment is reached,
> take refuge in the precious Buddha, who is the guru,
> take refuge in the holy Dharma, the teaching and realization,
> take refuge in the holy Sangha, the children of the
>   victorious ones.

Recite this refuge prayer as many times as possible, very mindfully. At the conclusion of the refuge, recite another prayer:

> May the precious Triple Gem bless my mind to proceed
>   toward the Dharma.
> Bless me to traverse the path of Dharma.
> Bless me to dispel errors on the path.
> Bless me that illusory visions may appear as primordial wisdom.
> Bless me that nonreligious thoughts may not appear for even
>   a moment.
> Bless me to attain buddhahood quickly.

This prayer mirrors the teachings of *Parting from the Four Attachments*. The first line, "May the precious Triple Gem bless my mind to proceed toward Dharma," parallels the first line of *Parting from the Four Attachments* that says, "If you have attachment to this life, you are not a religious person." To practice the true Dharma, we have to give up attachment to this life. This life is temporary, without essence, very fragile and impermanent, and therefore it has no meaning in itself. When we say, "May I proceed toward the Dharma," this means toward the real, true Dharma, not just what superficially appears to be Dharma. Dharma mixed with attachment to this life is still a worldly activity. At the beginning of our path, we pray to have our minds successfully proceed toward the Dharma.

The next line, "Bless me to traverse the path of the Dharma," means that although we may have entered the Dharma path, we are not properly upon the path unless renunciation arises. This is parallel to the line from *Parting from the Four Attachments*, "If you have attachment to the world of existence, you do not have renunciation." With this, we pray not only that we may enter the Dharma path, but also that we may enter with the proper renunciation.

The third line, "Bless me to dispel errors on the path," parallels the line, "If you have attachment to your own purpose, you do not have enlightenment mind." Even though we may have entered the path with proper renunciation, seeking liberation for ourselves alone is still an error. Even reaching the nirvana of self-liberation does not fully develop all of our good qualities and does not completely overcome all obscurations.

The next line, "Bless me that illusory visions may appear as primordial wisdom," is parallel to the fourth line in *Parting from the Four Attachments*, which says, "If grasping arises, you do not have the view." Because we lack wisdom, we are caught up in illusory visions. When wisdom arises, it transforms these illusory visions into primordial wisdom. In this way we pray to be able to successfully accomplish concentration meditation, or calm abiding (*shamatha*), and insight wisdom (*vipashyana*).

"Bless me that nonreligious thoughts may never be produced for even a moment" refers to all of the practices together. Because nonreligious thoughts lead to lower realms and samsara, we pray that they may never arise for even a single moment.

"Bless me to attain buddhahood quickly." The Mahayana path is the right practice; the correct practice; the path of all the past, present, and future buddhas. Once we enter it, we can quickly achieve buddhahood.

This concludes the first part of the preliminaries: changing from the wrong path to the right path.

Creation of enlightenment mind

The second part of the preliminary section of the teaching involves switching from the lower path to the higher path by generating enlightenment mind.

Buddhists believe in rebirth. This can be logically understood in the following way. We all have both a body and a mind. We can see and touch the physical body and describe its size, color, and shape. However, the mind is very different. We cannot see or touch it, or describe its color and shape. Because the body and mind are so very different, the mind cannot arise primarily from a physical body, from the elements, or from ordinary matter. It must arise from a continuity similar to itself.

We can describe where our physical bodies come from, how they are maintained, and how they will eventually be disposed of. But the mind cannot be disposed of in the way that we dispose of our physical body. The mind continues, and therefore it must come from the same type of continuity as itself. It must be a continuity that reaches back before our present body or life. If we go back from this life to the previous life, to the life before that and so on, there is no end. There is no original starting point.

This is what is meant by the phrase "since beginningless time." Each of our minds has continued since beginningless time. From beginningless time until now, we have been caught up in this cycle of existence. Since we have been here throughout beginningless time, there is not a single place where our body has not been born. There is not a single being that has not at one time been our very dear mother, father, and relatives.

Because of the changes that come with taking a new life, we no longer recognize each other. We see some of these dear ones as our enemies, some as our relatives, and some as neutral beings toward whom we are indifferent. But in reality, every single sentient being at one time or another has been our very dear relative, not only once but countless times. Each time, they gave us so much love, and cared for and benefited us just as our present dear ones have done.

Therefore, it is not right to seek liberation or enlightenment only for ourselves alone, ignoring the welfare of all these very dear mother sentient beings. We must care for them. The way to do this is to rescue them from the suffering of samsara and lead them to the path of happiness.

Because we are ordinary people, however, we have neither the freedom nor the ability to rescue them. Even powerful worldly deities and those who have already reached the nirvana of self-liberation do not have the power to save all sentient beings. Only fully enlightened buddhas can save all sentient beings. Therefore, for the benefit of all sentient beings, we wish to attain perfect enlightenment. This thought is known as enlightenment mind, or *bodhichitta*.

Enlightenment mind has two aspects: wishing enlightenment mind and engaging enlightenment mind. The wish to attain perfect enlightenment for the benefit of all sentient beings is known as wishing, or aspirational, enlightenment mind. The resolve to enact the vast and profound bodhisattva path to reach that goal is known as the engaging, or applied, enlightenment mind.

The actual recitation combines refuge and the creation of enlightenment mind with a dedication prayer. The prayer is:

In the Buddha, Dharma, and excellent Sangha,
I take refuge until enlightenment is reached.
Through deeds of giving and the like,
may I attain buddhahood for the sake of all sentient beings.

"Giving and the like" refers to the six bodhisattva perfections, or *paramitas*—generosity, moral conduct, patience, diligence, meditation, and wisdom.

Another recitation is: "I must attain buddhahood for the sake of all sentient beings. For that purpose I will diligently accomplish virtuous deeds of body, voice, and mind." In other words, the goal of all activities of body, voice, or mind is to attain enlightenment for the benefit of all sentient beings.

THE MAIN TEACHING

*If you have attachment to this life, you are not
a religious person.*

To practice this meditation, sit in a conducive place where there are
no external disturbances. Try to also avoid internal disturbances such
as conceptual thoughts. Sit cross-legged, and after reciting the refuge
and generating enlightenment mind, contemplate the first line of the
teaching, which is: "If you have attachment to this life, you are not a
religious person."

The general contents of this first line are common to the Hinayana,
Mahayana, and Vajrayana traditions. The first line directly describes
the right way and the wrong way to practice Dharma. Right Dharma
practice, pure Dharma practice, is not attached to this life. Practicing Dharma with attachment to this life is not real Dharma; it is still
worldly activity. Just like a mirage that appears to be water but does
not quench thirst, such activity is apparently Dharma but does not
liberate you from the sufferings of samsara.

If you practice Dharma with attachment to this life, any practice that
you do, whether it is moral conduct, study, contemplation, or meditation, will not even result in the accomplishment of prosperity in this
life. If the goal of Dharma practice is to gain fame, disciples, or wealth,
the practice will become the seed of the lower realms and samsara
instead of becoming the seed of liberation and enlightenment. It is not
actual Dharma practice. The great Indian master Vasubandhu said:

> Upon a base of sound moral conduct,
> hear, contemplate, and
> thoroughly apply yourself to meditation.

To be pure Dharma, whatever practice you do should not be mixed
with attachment to this life. This is because this life is very transient.

Very few people live longer than a hundred years. This life is also without essence: everything is impermanent and it is not really worthy of any attachment.

The goals of the Dharma path have many different levels. To say nothing of liberation or enlightenment, we should at minimum practice for a purpose beyond this life—in other words, at least for the benefit of our next life.

The first line of the teaching, "If you have attachment to this life, you are not a religious person," directly explains the right and wrong way to practice Dharma. Indirectly it points to the difficulty of obtaining a precious human birth endowed with the eighteen prerequisites. It also, because of impermanence, indicates the importance of diligently practicing Dharma without any delay.

Not only humans but every sentient being possesses buddha nature. The true nature of every sentient being's mind is unstained by obscurations. Any sentient being that meets with the right methods has the opportunity to become a fully enlightened buddha. However, among the six types of sentient beings, human beings have the best chance to accomplish buddhahood. Therefore, this human life, in particular one endowed with eighteen prerequisites, is very precious and difficult to find. As the great Indian master Shantideva says in *Engaging in the Conduct of the Bodhisattva* (1:4):

> These freedoms and endowments are very difficult to find,
> and they can accomplish the highest benefit of beings.
> If this benefit is not accomplished,
> how will they come about again?

First, we reflect on the difficulty of attaining this precious human birth. The prerequisites of precious human birth are difficult to attain from many points of view: based on their cause, number, examples, and nature.

Consider the difficulty of attaining a precious human birth based on its *cause*. The cause of a precious human life endowed with the prerequisites is the practice of virtuous deeds. In particular, the practice of virtue means abandoning nonvirtuous deeds and maintaining pure moral conduct. But when we look about samsara, most sentient beings are not engaged in virtuous deeds. The majority are indulging in nonvirtue, and many who appear to be engaged in virtuous deeds are engaged in only a superficial way.

Carefully reflect on your own actions from morning until night. How many negative thoughts arise? How many virtuous thoughts arise? Most people, if they examine their actions carefully and honestly, will notice that there are far more nonvirtuous thoughts and deeds than virtuous ones. Thus we realize that we only rarely accumulate pure virtue, which is the cause of obtaining a precious human birth endowed with the eighteen prerequisites. If the cause is only rarely accumulated, obviously the result of a precious human rebirth will very rarely be attained.

Next, consider the difficulty of attaining a precious human birth from the perspective of *number*. Although there are many human beings, humans are few in comparison to other types of beings. Although we talk about the population explosion, it is still possible to count the number of people in each country. However, it is impossible to count the number of insects even in a small space, such as a house. The number of humans is extremely small in proportion to all the other types of beings. In addition, not every human has a precious human life endowed with all the eighteen prerequisites, which is even rarer.

We can also consider the difficulty of attaining a precious human birth based on *examples*. Many examples, or metaphors, are given in the scriptures. One example compares the process of beings going to their next birth with throwing a handful of grain or lentils against a vertical wall. When the kernels hit the wall, virtually all fall down to the ground, which is like taking rebirth in the lower realms. Attaining a precious human birth endowed with the eighteen prerequisites is as likely as a lentil sticking to the wall.

Next, we reflect on the difficulty of attaining precious human birth from the point of view of its own *nature*.

The eighteen prerequisites

The nature of a precious human life is to be endowed with the eighteen prerequisites. The eighteen prerequisites consist of eight freedoms and ten endowments. The eight freedoms mean that we are free from rebirth in eight unfavorable states. Four of these are nonhuman states, and four are human states.

The four nonhuman states are birth among the beings in hell, hungry ghosts, animals, and long-lived gods. Beings born in the hell realms suffer greatly and have no opportunity to hear or practice Dharma. The situation is the same in the hungry ghost realm, where there is great hunger and thirst. The minds of beings in the animal realms are characterized by ignorance with no chance of understanding the Dharma. The fourth unfavorable state is rebirth as a long-lived god. There is a part of the form realm where only long-lived gods dwell. Other than birth and death, all of their mental activities have ceased, and they abide in a very high level of worldly meditation in which there is no opportunity to practice the true Dharma (because they do not experience suffering). These are the four unfavorable nonhuman births, where it is not possible to practice the Dharma.

Within the human realm, there are four unfavorable states. The first is birth among barbarians, who have no opportunity to even hear the word *Dharma*. Second is among people who hold wrong beliefs, such as those who may have heard the Dharma but do not accept its core beliefs, such as the law of karma, rebirth, and the like. The third unfavorable human state is birth in a world or time where a buddha has not appeared, so there is no Dharma to practice. Such a period is known as a "dark eon." A time during which a buddha has appeared is a "light eon." There are far more dark eons than light eons. The fourth unfavorable human state is birth as a person who is mentally or physically incapacitated so that even if they have an opportunity to receive the teachings, they are unable to perceive or comprehend them. These are the four unfavorable states of birth within the human realm.

There are ten endowments, or opportunities, that are necessary for your life to be considered a precious human birth. Five of these are acquired by yourself, and five are acquired from others. The five endowments acquired by yourself are: birth as a human, in a central realm, with sound sense organs, without having committed heinous crimes, and with sincere faith in the Buddha's teachings.

Birth as a human is the first endowment. The second is birth in a central realm. A realm is said to be central because it is geographically central, such as India, particularly Bodhgaya, where all the past, present, and future buddhas did and will accomplish enlightenment; or it is said to be central with respect to the Dharma because all four types of followers reside there: monks (*bhikshus*), nuns (*bhikshunis*), and male and female lay practitioners. The third endowment is to be born with sound sense organs, so that you can receive Dharma teachings and analyze and meditate on them. The fourth is not to have committed any of the five heinous crimes, those of killing one's mother, father, or an arhat, drawing blood from a buddha, or causing a schism in the Sangha. Purification of the five heinous crimes is very difficult through regular religious practices. The fifth endowment is sincere belief in the Buddha's teaching, particularly in the vinaya teachings on moral discipline, which are the root of the teachings. These are the five endowments that are acquired by yourself.

The five endowments that are acquired from others are: birth at a time during which a buddha has come into this world, when the buddha has bestowed the teachings, when the teachings continue to be upheld as a living tradition, when the followers are practicing, and when sponsors are supporting the Dharma.

Concerning the first of these endowments acquired from others, as I explained, there are far more dark eons than light eons. And even during the first part of a light eon, when peoples' lifespans are increasing, buddhas do not appear. They appear only during the latter part of the eon during the period of decreasing lifespans. Therefore, it is very rare for a buddha to appear in the world.

The second endowment is that having appeared, a buddha has bestowed the teachings. Buddhas do not turn the wheel of Dharma except for beings who are worthy and can comprehend the profound teachings.

The third endowment is that not only has a buddha bestowed the teachings but the teachings continue to be upheld as a living tradition. Many buddhas have appeared in this universe, but after a certain period of time, beings' memory of their teachings ends, and there are long gaps before another buddha appears.

The fourth endowment is that there are followers who can demonstrate a right example of how to practice the Dharma path. The fifth is that there are generous sponsors who support the Dharma through right livelihood unmixed with impure activities.

This is a summary of the ten endowments. Clearly, it is extremely difficult to attain a precious human birth, which includes freedom from all the eight unfavorable states and possession of all ten endowments simultaneously.

Such a precious human birth is not only very rare; it is also very precious, more precious, it is said, than a wish-fulfilling jewel. Supplicating a wish-fulfilling jewel can bestow material wealth, but it cannot bestow higher rebirth, personal liberation, or perfect enlightenment. However, by using our precious human life as a vehicle, we can reach higher rebirth; we can reach personal liberation; and we can even reach perfect enlightenment, buddhahood. This is why precious human birth is said to be even more precious than a wish-fulfilling jewel. Realizing that it is so precious and rare, we must not remain idle. We must diligently practice the holy Dharma.

Recalling then the first line of *Parting from the Four Attachments*, "If you have attachment to this life, you are not a religious person," we can see that it directly explains the right and wrong way to practice Dharma. Indirectly, it points to the difficulty of obtaining a precious human birth and the importance of diligently practicing Dharma without any delay.

Reflection on impermanence and death

Reflecting on impermanence and death helps us realize why we must practice the Dharma without delay. Everything that arises from causes and conditions is impermanent. This is particularly true of human life.

First, we contemplate the certainty of death. It is 100 percent certain that every being that is born in this universe will die. No one doubts that there was even a single being that was born but did not or will not die. Even noble buddhas and bodhisattvas, who in reality are beyond birth and death, manifest passing in the eyes of common people. Among ordinary people, whose birth is driven by karma and defilements, there is not a single person who was born but did not die. It is said:

All compounded things disintegrate.
The end of accumulation is exhaustion.
The end of gathering is separation.
The end of ascent to the heights is descent to the depths.
The end of birth is death.

Second, we contemplate the uncertainty of the time of death. No one can say how long he or she will live. We never know when death will occur. Looking around us, many beings die in the womb even before they are born. Some die at birth. Some die in infancy, and so on. No one knows for sure when they will die.

Although there are many external and internal conditions that shorten life, there are very few conditions that prolong life. Even those methods that usually prolong life, such as food and medicine, can also become the cause of death.

No one has a definite, fixed lifespan. Even supporting conditions such as youth, health, privilege, wealth, comfortable surroundings, and the like do not guarantee that you will live long. We all know healthy people who pass away suddenly before others who are chronically ill, young people who die before the aged, wealthy people with every facility and opportunity who die before the destitute who have nothing. Nothing can guarantee that any person will live for any certain duration of time.

Third, we contemplate that only the Dharma can benefit us at the time of death. All worldly wealth, power, fame, or knowledge is of no use in eluding death. At the time of death, the holy Dharma is the only thing upon which we can rely. We must practice diligently while we are still alive and have the benefits of relative youth and health. By devoting ourselves to the path of Dharma now, even if we cannot accomplish concrete results, at least we will not feel regret at the time of death.

By practicing the Dharma, we can have confidence that at least we will be born in a higher realm. Superior Dharma practitioners pass away with full confidence, as if they were returning to their own home. Middling practitioners face their death without hesitation. Lesser practitioners at least pass away without the regret that they have wasted their opportunity to practice the Dharma. Thinking of the certainty of death, and the uncertainty of the time of death, we must practice the Dharma immediately without delay.

Thus we have completed the explanation of the first line of the teaching, "If you have attachment to this life, you are not a religious person," which directly explains the right and wrong ways to practice Dharma, and indirectly explains the difficulty of obtaining precious human birth endowed with the eighteen prerequisites; impermanence; the inevitability of death; and finally the importance of practicing Dharma without delay and with great diligence.

If you have attachment to the world of existence, you do not have renunciation.

The second line, "If you have attachment to the world of existence, you do not have renunciation," means that if we are attached to the three realms—the desire realm, the form realm, and the formless realm—then Dharma practice does not lead us to enlightenment.

The first line, "If you have attachment to this life, you are not a religious person," explains that human life is not permanent; this current life will someday come to an end. When it does, our mental consciousness will not disappear; it will continue from life to life. Indulgence in nonvirtue will cause us to fall into the lower realms, where the suffering is immense. From fear of the suffering of the lower realms, we pray to always be reborn in the higher realms. For that to occur, we must practice virtuous deeds. It could be said that the first line explains what is known as the "small person's path," because although it is a spiritual path, it does not aim beyond the cycle of existence. The aim is to avoid falling into the lower realms and to be continuously reborn in the higher realms, such as the human realm or the gods' realms.

However, the second line explains that not only are the lower realms characterized by great suffering, but even in the higher realms there is no real happiness; there is nothing worthy of attachment. Therefore, we should develop renunciation, which is the thought to completely renounce the entirety of samsara. To develop renunciation, we must understand that all of samsara is suffering. When we realize this, real renunciation arises—we wish from the depths of our heart to renounce samsara and seek liberation.

Thus the teaching explains two main subjects: the faults of samsara, which produces renunciation, and the law of karma, or cause and effect, which explains how our own actions bind us within samsara.

The faults of samsara

The sutras state, "The desire realm has faults; likewise the form realm has faults; also the formless realm has faults. Only nirvana is faultless." If you wonder what kinds of faults or suffering are found in samsara, there are generally three types: the suffering of suffering, the suffering of change, and the suffering of the conditional nature of all phenomena.

The suffering of suffering

The first type of suffering is the suffering of suffering. This is that type of suffering that everyone normally considers to be suffering, such as physical pain and mental anxiety. Regarding this type of suffering, the sutras state, "Hell beings experience the fires of hell, hungry ghosts experience hunger and thirst, animals experience being devoured, humans experience short lives, and gods experience shamelessness. There is never any happiness upon the needle tip of existence." The suffering of suffering, then, is primarily experienced, and certainly most intensely, in the three lower realms: the hell realm, the hungry ghost realm, and the animal realm.

There are three types of hell realms: cold hells, hot hells, and neighboring or semi-hells. Among the cold hells, there are eight types.

The first cold hell is known as Blister Hell. From the power of their negative karma, hell beings are born miraculously, without developing in a womb, into the Blister Hell. The sky is completely dark; there is no sun and not even the light of a single star. Surrounded by snowy mountains covered with ice, stung by cold wind blowing from every direction, the hell beings have not even a patch of cloth to protect themselves from the cold. As the cold is so severe, the skin of their entire body naturally blisters, so it is called Blister Hell. This suffering is not short, as the lifespan of a being in this first hell realm is measured in the following way: Imagine a container filled with 3,500 pounds of sesame seeds, from which one seed is removed every hundred years. The lifespan of a being in Blister Hell is equal to the length of time it takes to completely empty the container, and beings must dwell there for that great length of time.

The second cold hell is called Bursting Blister Hell. The place and the nature of suffering are similar to the Blister Hell but twenty times colder. As a result, the hell beings' blisters burst, and water, pus, and blood leak from their bodies. The span of life in this realm is also twenty times longer than that in the previous one.

The third cold hell is called "Brrr" Hell because the cold is so severe that the beings there cannot speak but can only make the sound "Brrr."

The fourth cold hell is colder still, so that the voice does not work at all, and there is only the faint sound of exhaling air.

In the fifth cold hell, the cold is so severe that the beings' entire bodies are frozen. Because their teeth clench together, it is called Clenched Teeth Hell.

The sixth hell is far colder. The skin turns blue and cracks into eight parts, which causes the body to resemble the blue utpala flower. Therefore, it is called the Cracked Like an Utpala Hell.

In the seventh cold hell, strong gusts of wind cause the skin to crack open and the flesh underneath to crack further and turn red. The body then resembles a lotus. Therefore, this realm is called Cracked Like a Lotus Hell.

The eighth cold hell is even colder still. The body is completely frozen inside and out, so it becomes like a stone. Then it cracks into bits, and even the internal organs crack into pieces. As the cracked body resembles a large lotus flower, it is known as the Large Lotus Flower Hell.

Reflect on these realms, their sufferings, nature, and lifespan. Realize that there is no guarantee that we will not be born into such a place. The cause of these sufferings is performing nonvirtuous deeds in general, and in particular performing actions that cause other sentient beings and members of the Sangha to experience suffering from cold.

As we have already committed many nonvirtuous deeds, especially deeds performed in anger, there is no guarantee that we will not be reborn into such a place. That is why we must practice the holy Dharma now that we have been born as human beings with all of the necessary conditions.

In addition to the eight cold hells, there are eight hot hells. The first is called Reviving Hell. There, through the power of their karma, beings are miraculously born in an infant's body on a ground made of burning iron. Out of strong ego-clinging, whatever objects they pick up turn into weapons, any being that is perceived is seen as an enemy, and their minds are filled with anger. The guardians of hell chop their bodies into pieces and they collapse into unconsciousness. Then from the sky, a cool wind blows and the sound "revive" is heard. They regain consciousness, and the same process is repeated over and over. This is the first of the hot hells.

The second hot hell is called Black Line Hell. The guardians of that realm draw lines upon the bodies of the beings suffering there, just as carpenters mark a piece of wood, and then cut the body into many pieces.

The third hot hell is called the Crushing Hell. In this realm beings are born between burning mountains shaped like the heads of the animals they have slaughtered. They suffer greatly as their bodies are crushed between the burning iron mountains.

In the fourth hot hell, beings are born upon burning iron ground. Chased by hell guardians, they run into a nearby house hoping to escape. Upon entering the house, its doors close and lock so that there is no escape, and it becomes a house of burning iron. As they are burned by the fire, they suffer greatly and cry out, so it is called Crying Hell.

The fifth hot hell is called Great Crying Hell. It is similar to Crying Hell, except that instead of being trapped inside only one house, the beings are trapped inside two houses, one inside the other. If escape from the inner house were somehow possible, still there is no escape from the outer one. Therefore, the mental anguish is doubled, which is why it is called Greatly Crying Hell.

The sixth hell is known as Hot Hell. The guardians of this realm seize the beings born there and thrust a burning spear from the anus up to the crown of the head. The internal organs are completely burned by the blazing iron spear, and they suffer greatly.

The seventh is the Great Hot Hell. Instead of a single-pointed spear, a three-pronged trident is thrust into the anus and the prongs pierce the crown of the head and the right and left shoulders. Flames and smoke pour from the mouth and ears, and the beings there suffer terribly.

The eighth hot hell is called Unceasing, or Avici, Hell. There, beings burn inside an enormous iron stove, indistinguishable from the flames. Aside from their cries, there is no sign that any beings are suffering there. The suffering in this realm is the worst in samsara; there is no suffering greater than this.

The lifespans of beings in the first six hot hells are related to the lifespans of the gods in the highest level of the desire realm. As described in the *Treasury of the Abhidharma*, fifty human years is equivalent to one day of life in the lowest god realm, which is called the realm of the Four Guardian Kings. Counting fifty human years as one day, those gods live for five hundred of their own years. This entire five-hundred-year period is just one day in Reviving Hell. Calculating thus, hell beings live for five hundred of their own years.

Similarly, in the next higher god realm known as Thirty-Three, one thousand human years is equal to one day, and their lifespans are one thousand of their own years long. Continuing thus, based on the spans of life in each of the six god realms, the spans of life in each of the six hell realms increase in an almost unimaginable way. In the two lowest hells, the Great Hot Hell and Unceasing Hell, life lasts for half an intermediate eon and a full intermediate eon, respectively.

There are four types of neighboring hells. The first is called Fire Trench Hell. It is located at the perimeter of all of the other hells. If you are born in that hell, your limbs are burned whenever they touch the ground. When you lift your right foot, it is healed, while the left foot is burned. Likewise, the left foot it is healed when you lift it while the right one is burned.

The second neighboring hell is called Mud of Putrid Corpses Hell. The ground there is composed of impure things like rotting corpses and is so foul that ordinary beings would die merely from the odor. Their karma is such, however, that beings born in this realm do not easily die. In addition to the foul smell, within the mud are many worms with iron lips that eat into the limbs of beings born there and bore right down to the bones.

The third neighboring hell is called Path of Blades Hell, and it is divided into many sectors. Having crossed Mud of Putrid Corpses Hell, beings enter a plain of sharp, pointed knife blades. Walking there, the flesh and bones of their feet are cut into pieces, causing great suffering. Then they enter a forest of trees with sword-like branches and leaves. Having previously suffered greatly from the heat, they enter the forest seeking relief, but instead the leaves cut their bodies into many pieces. Next the beings see a mountain. While attempting to climb it their body is pierced by sharp, pointed iron spears. With great difficulty they finally reach the summit, but there many fearsome birds, such as ravens and kites with iron beaks, peck out their eyes and mouths and eat their brains. Hearing the voices of their relatives, they try to go back down the mountain to meet them, but in doing so, they again suffer from iron spears piercing their body. Finally they reach the base, but instead of meeting their relatives, iron jackals, dogs, and wolves eat their limbs and tear their bodies into many pieces. Also in this hell, if someone has lied and cheated others through nonvirtuous words, their tongue is stretched out over the burning iron ground, staked down by iron spikes, and then the hell guardians plow their tongue with sharp instruments. Thus they suffer greatly.

The fourth neighboring hell is called Uncrossable River of Hot Ash Hell. Having suffered greatly on the burning iron ground, and having crossed the plain of blades, they see a river in the distance and struggle to go there. When beings finally arrive and enter the river, the water turns into hot ashes. Their bodies are completely burned. When they try to escape, the river is surrounded by hell guardians who beat them back, and so they suffer.

In addition to the main hells and neighboring hells, there are also semi-hells with many different kinds of suffering. Because they are similar to the hell realms, they are called semi-hells. Some of these hells are actually located within the human realms. One example is animals that are boiled in hot water. There are many other types as well.

We must reflect on the suffering in these hell realms. These are not just stories; they are described in very authentic teachings given by the Buddha himself, as well as in many commentaries that describe in detail the sufferings of the hell realms, the conditions there, and the duration of lives there. We must reflect on them and make a very strong commitment to be free from such suffering and to free those who are suffering there through the practice of the holy Dharma.

The second lower realm is called the hungry ghost realm. Within that realm there are generally three types of hungry ghosts: those suffering from external obscurations, those suffering from internal obscurations, and those suffering from the obscuration of obscurations.

Beings are born in the realm of hungry ghosts through indulging in nonvirtuous deeds motivated by stinginess or greed. It is a deserted and depressing place, and just by seeing it, they feel very sad. Lacking even a single grain of food or drop of water, they suffer greatly from hunger and thirst for a long period of time. Sometimes hungry ghosts see in the distance a mountain of rice and a river and try to run there out of great hunger. When they arrive, however, they find white rocks instead of rice and blue slate or nothing at all instead of water. As their bodies are very weak and skeletal, they endure great difficulty in running to the mirage, and when they realize that there is no food there at all, they experience even greater suffering. These are the sufferings of hungry ghosts with external obscurations.

The second type of hungry ghost is those with internal obscurations. These beings occasionally find a little bit of filthy food, such as mucus or pus. Out of great hunger they try to eat it, but it cannot fit into their mouths, which are as tiny as the eye of a needle. When some filth finally enters, their mouths tear and bleed, yet still the food sticks in their throats, which are as thin as the hair of a horse's tail. Eventually passing through their throats into their huge stomachs, the bit of filth disappears, and instead of satisfying their hunger, it makes them even hungrier.

The third type of hungry ghost suffers from the obscuration of obscurations. They search everywhere for food, but instead of finding it they are chased by the overseers of the hungry ghost realm who beat them and cause them to suffer. Sometimes they may find a little bit of filth such as mucus, but it is very difficult for them to swallow it. If they manage to swallow a little bit, when it reaches their stomachs it becomes fire; instead of satisfying their hunger, it burns the inside of their bodies.

Until their karma is exhausted, hungry ghosts suffer in these ways and cannot escape from the hungry ghost realm. We must reflect on their suffering and resolve to practice Dharma so that we will not be born into that realm.

The third lower realm is the animal realm. Generally, there are two main types of animals: those dwelling in the ocean and those scattered about on land.

For those animals that dwell in the ocean, life is very difficult. Wherever the ocean's waves take them, they must go. Thus, their dwelling place and companions are constantly changing. Some areas are in such complete darkness that the animals cannot even see their own extremities. Wherever they go, they are always afraid of being eaten. Sometimes many small ones eat a single large one; sometimes a single large one eats many small ones. Also, human beings catch and slaughter them. Because these animals are always afraid of being eaten, they must constantly be alert and so they never have a single moment of relaxation.

Among those animals that are scattered about on land, there are two types: those that belong to or depend upon human beings and those that are undomesticated. Those that belong to human beings must pull heavy carts, plow fields, and submit to milking. They are tied with iron chains and beaten with sticks and hooks. They are forced to perform many types of hard work. At the end of their lives, when they are old, instead of being retired they are killed for their flesh and bones. Those animals that are scattered about on land but are undomesticated must always be alert, for they are constantly hunted by human beings and other animals. Chased by hunters' dogs, they try to run away but fall down and are killed for their flesh, skin, bones, or horns.

All animals live with complete ignorance, just as if a huge rock were placed over their heads, and they have no notion of what is right and what is wrong. In addition, animals also endure many other types of suffering not described here.

The suffering of change

The second type of suffering is the suffering of change. The suffering of change is based on those feelings that we normally consider to be pleasurable. Due to impermanence, the seed of suffering exists within them, for when the pleasure ceases, we suffer. When compared to the suffering of the lower realms, they do seem pleasurable, but in reality they are another kind of suffering. The suffering of change is mainly found in the higher realms, particularly in the god realms.

Because of their good karma, beings are born into the god realms with beautiful bodies. They live in luxurious places with fine clothes and limitless enjoyments. But this is not permanent. Although the gods have very long lives, they are absorbed in enjoyments, so their life goes by very quickly. Suddenly, the signs of death appear. Their flower garlands wilt, their bodies lose their radiant beauty, and for the first time they appear dirty and their clothes are sweaty. They realize that they will soon have to face death, and through their clairvoyance they also foresee where they will be reborn. Having spent their entire lives in enjoyment, they have neglected serious Dharma practice. Therefore, they usually fall into the lower realms where there is an unimaginable amount of physical suffering. Foreseeing this, they experience enormous mental agony—even greater than the physical suffering of the hell realms.

Gods in the higher realms such as the form realm and formless realm do not have much physical suffering. However, no matter how high a bird flies in the sky, it must eventually land on the ground. In the same way, although these gods have reached a very high level of worldly meditation, the power of their meditation is eventually exhausted, and because they did not accomplish liberation, they fall down again into the lower realms. However high you go in samsara, you cannot remain there permanently, and you will inevitably fall down again.

The demigods are always competing with the gods on the battlefield, yet due to their inferior merit, they are always defeated. All of the males are killed on the battlefield, and seeing this, all of the females suffer greatly.

Among human beings, there is no one who is free from the four major sufferings of birth, aging, sickness, and death. In addition to these, there are many other kinds of suffering, such as not being able to fulfill our wishes, fear of being separated from our dear ones, fear of meeting our enemies, and so on.

Therefore, in the entirety of samsara—not only in the lower realms, but also on the highest peaks of samsara—there is nothing worthy of attachment.

The suffering of the conditional nature of all phenomena
The third type of suffering, the suffering of the conditional nature of all phenomena, describes those feelings usually considered to be neutral; they are seemingly neither pleasurable nor painful. An example of this is dissatisfaction. Wherever you go, with whomever you associate, whatever activities you engage in, there is no satisfaction. There is always something to complain about.

All of these types of suffering demonstrate that our very existence in samsara is suffering. In brief, as long as we remain within these six realms of existence, there is no freedom from suffering. Just as the nature of fire is hot whether the fire is small or large, so similarly the nature of samsara is suffering. Therefore, make a very serious resolve to practice the pure Dharma so that you will be freed not only from the suffering of the lower realms but from samsara in its entirety.

The law of karma

Next reflect on the law of karma, or cause and effect. The reason we are caught up in samsara is that we have indulged in nonvirtuous deeds. To free ourselves from suffering, we must abandon the causes of suffering. We must abandon nonvirtuous deeds and try to practice virtuous deeds. The next sections explain nonvirtuous deeds, virtuous deeds, and neutral deeds.

Nonvirtuous deeds and their results

What are nonvirtuous deeds? Any actions that are caused by negative emotions or defilements are nonvirtuous deeds. We will identify nonvirtuous deeds, and then we will consider the types of suffering resulting from indulging in these deeds and how to abandon them.

Nonvirtuous deeds are often described in a list of ten. The first is killing, whether from anger, desire, or ignorance. Killing your enemy is an example of killing out of anger. Killing animals for the sake of flesh or skin is an example of killing out of desire. Small children or adults killing animals for pleasure while hunting or in sport is an example of killing out of ignorance. In any case, whether the main cause is desire, anger, or ignorance, killing any living being from a tiny insect up to a god or human being, through any of the various methods such as weapons or poison, or even requesting another to do the killing, is the number one nonvirtuous deed.

The second is stealing. Stealing is the act of taking another's possessions for yourself without the other's permission. This includes stealing very insignificant things up to very precious things, whether forcefully or quietly, through cheating or by any other method.

The third is sexual misconduct. This means to engage in any kind of sexual activity with someone other than your legal partner.

These first three nonvirtuous deeds are committed with the body. The next four are committed with the voice.

The fourth nonvirtuous deed is lying. To tell another something that is not true for the purpose of deception is lying.

The fifth is calumny, speech that creates disharmony—speaking words, whether they are false or true, that incite discord between individuals or groups.

The sixth is harsh speech. This is using very sharp words, out of anger or another negative emotion, that cause the listener to feel pain just by hearing them.

The seventh is idle talk or irrelevant speech. This is to talk about subjects that are not beneficial but instead increase defilements such as desire, anger, and jealousy.

These are the four nonvirtues that are committed through speech. The next three are committed with the mind.

The eighth nonvirtuous deed is covetousness. Covetousness occurs when, upon seeing the wealth or power of another, desire arises in the mind to obtain that property or power for yourself.

The ninth is ill will or malicious thoughts. Ill will is a wish, stemming from hatred, that someone else will experience suffering or die.

The tenth nonvirtuous deed is wrong view. This means not believing in the law of karma, in rebirth, or in the authentic teachings because of ignorance.

Consider the temporary and ultimate results of indulging in these nonvirtuous deeds. The temporary result is similar to the action that was performed. For example, those who slaughter animals or kill human beings will have a very short life. By creating pain in another's body, they will have a very unhealthy life; by stealing the wealth of others they will experience poverty; by engaging in sexual misconduct they will experience very unhappy marriages.

By engaging in any of these nonvirtuous deeds, you will experience a result that is similar to the cause. In this life you will have such undesirable experiences and in the next life you will experience a result based on the amount of nonvirtue that was performed, as well as the defilement that was the motivation. For example, killing someone out of anger has a very strong result, so someone who performs such an act will most likely fall into the hell realms. Someone who slaughters animals or other beings out of desire, such as desire for their wealth, will most likely fall into the hungry ghost realm. Someone who slaughters animals or other beings out of ignorance, such as for fun or enjoyment, will most likely fall into the animal realm.

Carefully consider how to abandon these nonvirtuous deeds. By indulging in nonvirtuous deeds, all that you gain is suffering in this life and the causes of suffering in the lower realms in future lives. In this way, indulging in nonvirtuous deeds is the greatest harm that you can inflict upon yourself, so with a very strong will, resolve to abandon them. Then having made this resolution, abstain from nonvirtuous deeds.

Virtuous deeds and their results

Next consider virtuous deeds. What are the virtuous deeds? Virtuous deeds are the opposite of the ten nonvirtuous deeds. They are abstaining from killing, abstaining from stealing, abstaining from sexual misconduct, and so on. These ten acts, when performed without the influence of the defilements, are virtuous deeds.

Practicing these virtuous deeds brings about the experience of all positive temporal and ultimate results. By abstaining from killing, you will have a very long and healthy life; by abstaining from stealing you will have great wealth; by abstaining from sexual misconduct you will have a happy marriage, and so on. In this way, you will experience all the opposite temporal results of performing the nonvirtuous deeds.

The ultimate result depends on the amount of virtue that is

performed. If it is a small, medium, or large amount, you will accomplish one of the three enlightenments, such as that of the shravakas, pratyekabuddhas, or bodhisattvas. Practicing these virtuous deeds accomplishes ultimate happiness and brings about the fulfillment of all wishes. Practicing even small virtuous deeds can accomplish the great result of the shravaka or pratyekabuddha stage, which is completely free from all suffering. Therefore, resolve with a very strong will to practice even tiny virtuous deeds and then perform them diligently.

Neutral deeds

Next consider neutral deeds. Neutral deeds are deeds that are performed without the influence of either strong defilements or virtuous attitudes. Activities such as sleeping, eating, and walking are examples of neutral deeds. Neutral deeds produce results that are neither positive nor negative. They are better than nonvirtuous deeds because they do not produce any obvious suffering, but because they also do not produce any positive results, they are a waste of time.

When considering any deed, its motivation is the most important factor. Transforming our motivation can change neutral deeds into virtuous deeds. For example, eating food is normally a neutral deed, but if we eat food with the motivation to stay alive so that we can devote our lives to practicing virtuous deeds or to practicing the holy Dharma, then the neutral act of eating is transformed into a virtuous deed. Other deeds can be transformed in a similar way. Traveling is transformed into a virtuous deed by praying to meet our spiritual master, to meet the Buddha, or to hear the Dharma. Changing our motivation can transform all neutral deeds into virtuous deeds.

This completes the teaching on the second line of the teaching, "If you have attachment to the realm of existence, you do not have renunciation." It explains the faults of samsara, from the hell realms up to the god realms. Also, it explains the reason we are currently dwelling within samsara through its explanation of the law of karma.

If you have attachment to your own purpose, you do not have enlightenment mind.

Before we begin the third line, I would like to briefly summarize the meaning of the first two lines.

The first line is, "If you have attachment to this life, you are not a religious person." This shows the path to avoid the terrible suffering of the lower realms and to be continuously reborn in the higher realms. To follow this path, we need to abandon all nonvirtuous deeds and to diligently practice virtuous deeds. This path is called the small person's path because its goal is still within the cycle of existence; thus it is a very basic or rudimentary spiritual path.

The second line of the teaching is, "If you have attachment to the world of existence, you do not have renunciation." This explains that suffering exists not only in the lower realms but also in the higher realms. The higher realms appear to be a mixture of suffering and happiness. But in reality it is all suffering, because everything is impermanent. All compounded phenomena are impermanent, and all things that are impermanent have the nature of suffering. In order to develop the wish to be completely free from every part of samsara, it is necessary to develop renunciation. In order to develop renunciation, the teachings associated with the second line explain in detail both the suffering of samsara and the reason we are caught up in samsara, which is the law of cause and effect. When we realize that the entirety of samsara is nothing but suffering, then we no longer have any wish or place to stay, just as when a lake is frozen, swans have no place to stay, or when a forest is burned, birds have no place to stay. Thus, realizing that the entirety of samsara is nothing but suffering, we very sincerely and wholeheartedly wish to attain liberation. This type of path, where liberation is sought for one's own self, is called the middle person's path.

The third line is, "If you have attachment to your own purpose, you do not have enlightenment mind." Based on the second line, we realized that all of the worlds of existence are nothing but suffering, and we developed the sincere wish to be free from those experiences. In setting out to accomplish that result, we perform many lesser and middling virtuous deeds and finally achieve the state of personal liberation, which is the realization of the pratyekabuddhas and shravakas. These two types of personal liberation are great in the sense that all gross suffering and its causes have been completely eliminated.

Personal liberation, however, is not the final goal. Although personal liberation is great compared to samsara because one who attains that level is free from suffering, all of the good qualities are not fully developed because only the obscuration of the defilements has been removed. The state of personal liberation is still limited by the obscuration of knowledge, which blocks the achievement of full enlightenment. Because the good qualities of those on the stage of personal liberation are not developed to their fullest potential, they cannot benefit other sentient beings, and thus neither their own nor others' purposes are fulfilled. Attaining personal liberation also hinders accomplishing full enlightenment, because having reached that state, beings remain there for a very long time. If you build a house, it is difficult to tear it down and rebuild it again in a different way. Likewise personal liberation is really the greatest obstacle to accomplishing full enlightenment.

Once when Lord Buddha was in India, his disciple Ananda was about to give a teaching to five hundred disciples. Just before he began, Manjushri appeared. Ananda requested Manjushri to give the teaching instead. It is said that if Ananda had given the teaching, all five hundred disciples would have achieved the nirvana of personal liberation. After Manjushri gave the teaching, however, it became apparent that all five hundred disciples would be reborn in the hell realms. Seeing this, Ananda reported to the Buddha, "Today, Manjushri did something very bad. If I had given the teaching, all of the disciples would have accomplished nirvana. But because of Manjushri's teaching, now they will all fall into the hell realms." The Buddha replied, "What Manjushri did was right. If you had given the teaching, they would have accomplished nirvana, but it would have been very difficult for them to achieve full enlightenment; it would have taken a very long time. Thanks to Manjushri's teaching, all of their negative karma ripened very quickly, so although they will fall into the hell realms, they will begin the path toward full enlightenment and reach the highest attainment faster than they otherwise would have."

This story shows that it is not right to seek liberation only for our own purpose. The goal for which we all should aim is full enlightenment for the benefit of all beings. Such enlightenment does not arise without a cause, from an incomplete cause, or from the wrong cause and condition. For example, if we plant a rice seed during the winter, then although the correct seed was planted, still rice will not grow. Likewise, if we plant a wheat seed, rice will not appear. To grow rice, we need a rice seed as well as the proper temperature, moisture, and time. All of the correct causes and conditions must be present in order for the rice to grow.

In a similar way, accomplishing full enlightenment requires the proper seed, the proper cause, and all of the necessary conditions. As it is said in the *Mahavairochana Tantra*, "The root cause of enlightenment is great compassion, and the conditions are enlightenment mind and the performance of skillful means." Possessing the root cause, the conditions, and performing skillful means, we will accomplish full enlightenment. In order to accomplish these three, we need to meditate on loving kindness, compassion, and enlightenment mind, and to observe the precepts of the bodhisattva's conduct.

Loving kindness

First we need to develop loving kindness. In the beginning, it is difficult for most of us to develop loving kindness toward all sentient beings. For this reason, the pith instructions include four steps for developing loving kindness.

The first step is to meditate on loving kindness for our relatives, who are objects of attachment and toward whom we can more easily develop loving kindness. The second step is to meditate on those toward whom we are indifferent, who are considered to be the objects of ignorance. The third and more difficult step is to meditate on loving kindness toward our enemies, who are the objects of our anger. The fourth step is to meditate on loving kindness for all sentient beings indiscriminately.

To practice the first step, which is meditation on loving kindness toward our relatives, our mother is often recommended as the object of meditation. This is because our mother gave us life, gave us our very bodies, and taught us at a young age what is right and wrong, among many other things. Nonetheless, we can meditate on whatever friend or relative is dearest.

The first step has three stages: first recall your mother or dearest one, then remember her kindness, and finally meditate on loving kindness toward her. So first, think, "She has been my mother not only in this life but in many other previous lifetimes." We have been caught in samsara since beginningless time, have lived innumerable lives, and so have had countless mothers. As Nagarjuna said, "Even if you had pills the size of juniper seeds equalling the extent of the earth, the number of pills would still not equal the number of mothers you have had." It is also said in the sutras, "There is not enough water in the four oceans to equal the amount of milk that your mothers have given you." Not only in this life, but in innumerable lifetimes, she has given us so much milk.

In addition to being our mother, she has also been other relatives, such as our father, brother, sister, and so on. It is said that if those who have been our father were stacked one upon another like horses or elephants, they would tower over the world of Brahma. All of the gifts that we have received from these relatives would also tower over Brahma's realm.

The second stage is to remember our mother's kindness. Her first act of kindness was giving us a body. After carrying our body around in her womb for nine or ten months and enduring the strains of heaviness and fatigue, she endured the pain of giving birth, even risking her own life. Her second kindness was giving us life. After being born, we were just like a tiny worm that does not know anything and cannot do anything. With a loving heart, she protected us from fire, water, and danger, looked upon us with loving eyes, fed us with food from her own tongue, and cleaned dirt from our body with her own hands. Because babies are unable to survive by themselves, if she had not cared for us, we would surely have died. But she did not let us die, thus her second kindness was in giving us life.

Our mother gave all of her most precious possessions and even risked her life for the benefit of us, her children, as we grew up. She also taught all different types of knowledge and tried to establish us in human society on an equal footing with everyone else. Children know almost nothing, but she taught us everything, including how to talk and how to act. Today, each of us has grown up, is able to receive the precious teachings, and has the opportunity to practice the Dharma thanks to our mother's kindness. Without her kindness and care we would not have such opportunities. It is said in some commentaries that our first guru in life is our mother.

Thus remember that at the very beginning of this life our mothers gave us our life, gave us our body, and even up to this very moment have given us so much else. In addition to their kindness in this life, they have similarly given so much benefit, so much love, and so much care in many past lives. In this way, remember your mothers' kindness.

Then the third stage is to meditate on loving kindness. What is loving kindness? On the most basic level, it is the mind that wishes for another's happiness. Loving kindness was described thus by the great Indian master Chandrakirti, "Great loving kindness is said to be a way to accomplish benefit for sentient beings." After recalling our mother and remembering her kindness, we then seek to pay back all of the kindness, benefit, and care that she has given. The way to benefit our mother is to make her happy—physically happy, mentally happy, and possessing all the causes of happiness.

To do this, first generate loving kindness that is linked with enlightenment mind. Think, "I must help my kind mother to be happy and to have the causes of future happiness." Then generate loving kindness that is linked with intention by thinking, "I wish that she may be happy and have the causes of happiness." After that, generate loving kindness that is linked with a prayer by praying, "May the guru and Triple Gem help my mother to be happy and to have the causes of happiness."

In this way, first practice loving kindness toward your mother or toward whomever you feel closest. After practicing with the closest relative, expand the practice to include other relatives, friends, neighbors, or people with whom you have connections.

The second step is to meditate on loving kindness toward those beings with whom you are indifferent. This includes all beings with whom you have no connection, good or bad—the countless sentient beings that you have never seen or heard. It is important to practice loving kindness toward them because although they appear as strangers at the moment, they are also our own previous mothers, fathers, and relatives. As we have discussed, we have been caught in samsara since beginningless time and have lived countless lives. Throughout that time, these beings to whom we are currently indifferent have often been our mothers or fathers. At that time, they gave us the same care and the same benefit that our present mother has given us in this life. Therefore, we must generate loving kindness toward them in the same way that we practiced it with our current mother or dear ones.

The third and more difficult step is to meditate on loving kindness for our enemies or those who cause obstacles for us. This practice is important because the same people who today appear as our most hated enemies are in reality our own previous mothers, fathers, and dear ones. Because we are now in a new life, we cannot recognize the people from our past lives. Seeing each other now as enemies, we bring each other great suffering. But we should recognize that these enemies have been very kind to us in the past.

In addition they also bring us great benefit in the current life, because by appearing as our enemies, they crush our pride and bring us the opportunity to develop patience. They also give us the chance to pay back all of the kindness and benefit that they showed us in previous lives. Their appearance as enemies is none other than a claim to receive in return the love and benefit that they gave us so often in the past.

The final step is to meditate on loving kindness toward all sentient beings without any exception or discrimination. Practice in the same way as before, focusing on all sentient beings of the six realms. First recognize them as your mothers, then remember their kindness, and finally repay them by generating loving kindness. Practice in this way until a genuine and natural feeling of loving kindness toward all sentient beings arises in your mind.

If while doing this practice your mind feels anger toward your enemies and you cannot develop loving kindness, remember that anger creates much more harm for yourself than for your enemy. The only way to avoid that harm is to overcome anger, and the only way to overcome anger is through the practice of loving kindness. In this way, remember the consequences you will face by indulging in anger, remember all of the benefits of practicing loving kindness, and thus generate genuine loving kindness.

The sutras state, "It is far more meritorious to practice a single moment of loving kindness toward sentient beings than to make offerings vast enough to fill the entire universe."

Compassion

Thus having well trained the mind in loving kindness, next practice compassion. The reason we practice loving kindness before practicing compassion is that in order for compassion toward sentient beings to arise, we must first see them as lovable, for example by seeing them as our mothers. If we cannot first see them as lovable, compassion will not arise. When we become able to see all of them as our mothers or dear ones, then we become able to wish them to be happy and to have the causes of happiness.

After generating this wish, if we then examine the nature of samsara, we see that sentient beings actually lack happiness. The majority of beings are experiencing great suffering, and out of ignorance they are also creating the causes of even more future suffering. When we can see that all mother sentient beings suffer, then compassion arises. Thus loving kindness serves as the path to compassion, and compassion arises based on understanding suffering.

You may wonder, "What exactly is compassion?" Chandrakirti stated, "Completely saving beings who are experiencing suffering is great compassion." As Chandrakirti explained, having seen unbearable suffering, that mind that wishes beings to be freed from it is called compassion.

Compassion is developed by practicing step by step. The steps to practicing compassion are similar to the four stages in the practice of loving kindness. The first stage is to meditate on compassion for relatives, then for indifferent beings, then for enemies, and finally for all sentient beings.

In practicing compassion toward our relatives, start as before by recollecting your mother and remembering her kindness. Visualize your mother, whether she is alive or deceased, in front of yourself, and think, "Because my very kind mother is suffering and without happiness, I must have compassion for her."

Although she desires to be free from suffering and the causes of suffering, you can see that her present condition is suffering and is creating the causes of future suffering. Then think, "I must free my mother from such suffering and its causes." After meditating on this, link that thought with enlightenment mind, and then with intention, and finally with the prayer to the gurus and the Triple Gem that your mother may be free from suffering and its causes. You may focus on whichever of these three methods is most effective for your own mind.

After performing this meditation on compassion for your mother, again expand the focus to include other relatives, friends, and neighbors, beings toward whom you are indifferent, enemies, and finally all sentient beings. Practice in this way until a genuine inner feeling of compassion arises—not contrived compassion, but natural heartfelt compassion for all sentient beings without exception. The cultivation of compassion by this method will in turn help enlightenment mind to arise.

Enlightenment mind

Even though we may sincerely wish that all sentient beings be happy and free of suffering, in reality the opposite is happening: every sentient being continues to suffer. Seeing this, if we have loving kindness and compassion, we cannot remain idle. We need to make efforts to rescue sentient beings from the suffering of samsara. At the moment, however, we lack the knowledge, the skill, and the power to do so. We are completely bound by our own karma and defilements; we are blown about helplessly by the winds of karma. Just as a crippled mother is powerless to save her child from a burning building, in the same way we are unable to rescue sentient beings from samsara. This is true not only for us, but also for very powerful worldly deities such as Brahma and Indra, and even for the shravakas and prateykabuddhas who have already reached nirvana. None of them are able to save sentient beings.

Who is it that can save sentient beings? Only fully enlightened buddhas are able to do so. Just a single ray of light shining from a buddha's body can save countless sentient beings in a single moment. Understanding this, a profound urge arises within us to attain full enlightenment for the benefit of all sentient beings. This sincere wish is known as *wishing enlightenment mind*. Having made that wish, all of the efforts we exert in fulfilling it are known as *entering* or *engaging enlightenment mind*.

From beginningless time up until this moment, we have cared solely for ourselves and worked solely for our own benefit. Every exertion we have performed was for our own benefit alone. But by acting in this way, all we have actually accomplished is more and more suffering. So this time, instead of caring for ourselves, we must care for others. As Shantideva says in *Engaging in the Conduct of the Bodhisattva* (8:129), "All the suffering that beings experience in this universe arises from caring for the self alone, and all the happiness that beings experience in this world arises from caring for others." If we had already practiced caring for others in our previous lives, we would not still be in samsara—we would have already attained liberation and enlightenment. The reason we have not cared for others is our natural tendency to care for ourselves. This is a very gross mistake. The way to correct it is to ignore ourselves and to totally devote our energy and efforts to benefiting other sentient beings.

When developing enlightenment mind, it is important to proceed step by step, as before. We have spent so many lifetimes caring for ourselves alone that regardless of how much we like or love other beings, there is still a sense of difference between ourselves and others—our number one concern is still ourselves. The first step, therefore, is to train in viewing others as equal to ourselves. Think that just as we wish to be free from suffering, so, too, all other sentient beings have the same feeling, the same wish. Because other sentient beings have the same wish, just seeking happiness for self alone is not right. In this way, view other sentient beings as equal in importance to ourselves.

After we have become accomplished in this, then proceed with the meditation of exchange. This meditation is called *tonglen* in the Tibetan language. *Tong* means to give and *len* means to take. In this practice, instead of caring for ourselves, we care for others. We take all of the physical pains and mental sufferings of sentient beings as vast as space onto ourselves. In return, we give our own body, wealth, and virtuous deeds of the past, present, and future, without any attachment or clinging, to all other beings. While performing this exchange, we recite the words that accompany the meditation. Performing this practice crushes self-cherishing and self-clinging. Taking all of the suffering of sentient beings onto ourselves and sincerely wishing for their benefit accumulates great merit. In this way, we ourselves actually receive the most immediate benefit of this practice. This exchange meditation is one of the main practices of a bodhisattva.

The bodhisattvas' conduct

Another main practice of a bodhisattva is to preserve the precepts. In a general sense, the practice or behavior of a bodhisattva is to abandon harming others and to benefit them as much as possible. In particular, a bodhisattva's main practice is the six perfections: generosity, moral conduct, patience, diligence, meditation, and wisdom. Practice of these perfections cultivates the good qualities of mind. The first five are included in the method aspect of the path, while the sixth is the wisdom aspect.

Of the six perfections, wisdom is the most important. If the other perfections are performed without being linked to wisdom, the actions are just ordinary virtuous deeds and not "perfect" at all. However, when they are linked with wisdom, they become perfections. In order to link the other perfections with wisdom, abandon clinging to what are known as the three cycles. In the example of generosity, the three cycles are the *recipient*, such as a beggar, the *giver*, such as yourself, and *that which is given*, such as food or clothing. As long as there is clinging to these three cycles as separate and ultimately real, even though an action may be truly generous, you are not performing the *perfection* of generosity.

Understand that at the relative level, the three cycles exist, but on the ultimate level, they do not. In reality there is no recipient, no giver, and nothing that is given. All are like an illusion or a dream. In dreams we see an object, a subject, and other things, but when we awaken, all of these are gone without a trace. Similarly, the three cycles appear like an illusion but in reality they cannot be found.

Wisdom that does not cling to the three cycles is known as the perfection of wisdom. When the other perfections—generosity, moral conduct, patience, diligence, and meditation—are linked with this wisdom, they become perfections, which are the actual cause of attaining full enlightenment. Put another way, when the other perfections are devoid of wisdom, they are like a blind person; the perfection of wisdom is like a person with sight. When a person with sight leads a blind person, both of them progress toward full enlightenment.

Practicing these six perfections matures the good qualities of our own minds. In addition, there are other practices, such as the four means of gathering adherents and bringing their minds to maturation: the practices of giving, speaking pleasantly, encouraging others to practice, and practicing very diligently yourself. Detailed explanations of these may be found in many great commentaries, such as the *Essence of Space (Akashagarbha) Sutra*, Shantideva's *Compendium of Buddhist Precepts*, his *Engaging in the Conduct of the Bodhisattva*, and Nagarjuna's *Jewel Garland*, among others.

This completes the explanation of the third line of *Parting from the Four Attachments*, which explains the entire bodhisattva's path of seeking full enlightenment for the benefit of all sentient beings. Therefore, this is known as the great person's path.

If grasping arises, you do not have the view.

The fourth line, "If grasping arises, you do not have the view," means that although we have now developed relative enlightenment mind based on the practice of the third line, we still cling to phenomena as real. As a result, we fall into either the extreme of eternalism or the extreme of nihilism. As long as we remain in these extremes, we cannot accomplish enlightenment. In order to overcome such grasping at substantiality and essential characteristics, we must meditate on calm abiding (*shamatha*) and insight wisdom (*vipashyana*). The actual method of eliminating the defilements is through the practice of insight wisdom. Before practicing insight wisdom, however, we must first develop a base of calm abiding, or concentration. All together, the practice of the fourth line includes three stages: meditation on calm abiding, meditation on insight wisdom, and meditation on the combination of these two.

Calm abiding

It is necessary to do calm-abiding meditation before attempting to practice insight wisdom, because at the moment our minds are very busy with many streams of thoughts. With such a busy mind, we will be unable to meditate properly on insight wisdom.

To meditate on calm abiding, we need to find a place that is free of what are called the thorns of meditation, namely a place free of external and internal disturbances that hinder practice. It should be a secluded place pleasing to the mind. There, begin with the preliminary practices such as taking refuge and generating enlightenment mind, just as we do in all meditation sessions. Then, if you are able, sit in the vajra position, also known as the lotus position: the two feet crossed, two hands in meditation posture, the tip of the tongue lightly touching the palate, the spine straight, and the eyes half closed. Thus meditate in the proper position.

There are many different ways of practicing calm-abiding meditation, including many types of concentrations on outer objects and inner objects. For beginners, it is easier and more appropriate to focus on outer objects. Among the many outer objects it is possible to focus on, the best is an image or statue of the Buddha. By focusing on an image of the Buddha, we not only develop concentration; we also accumulate great merit.

If you choose to meditate on a mental image of the Buddha, then visualize a golden Shakyamuni Buddha seated on a jeweled throne upon a lotus and moon disc. His right hand is in the earth-touching gesture and his left hand is in meditation posture face up in his lap. He is wearing the three robes of a fully ordained monk and sitting in the full vajra position, his feet face up on the opposing knees. Either by looking at a statue, or visualizing very clearly, focus on the body in general, and particularly on the space between the eyebrows, where there is a white hair curled in a spiral. Then, instead of looking at the various colors and shapes of the visualization or statue, try to bring your mind, eyes, and breath together and remain focused on that single spot without any distractions.

In trying to develop calm-abiding meditation, it is said that there are five faults that hinder the practice. Fortunately, there are eight antidotes to counter these five faults. Finally, there are nine methods to aid the meditation. Of the five faults, the main one is laziness or unwillingness to do the meditation. The antidote to laziness is recollecting the benefits of calm-abiding meditation. Try to develop sincere faith that through this meditation, you will accomplish mundane attainments, such as physical and mental well-being and bliss, as well as the ultimate attainment of enlightenment.

If you meditate with a steady body, a steady object of meditation, no blinking, and no bending of the body, the first experience that will arise is the perception that even more streams of thoughts are arising in the mind than before. In fact these streams of thoughts are always present in the mind, one after another, but normally we are so busy with other activities that we do not recognize them. When we sit down and try to concentrate, then we see the thoughts arising. Seeing the thoughts arising is actually a positive sign, so do not feel discouraged.

By continuously practicing in this way, you will slowly be able to reduce the number of thoughts in the mind. Eventually, with the right conditions and sufficient merit, you will be able to remain single-pointedly in complete tranquility without any disturbances or thoughts. This is the attainment of calm abiding.

Insight wisdom

Calm-abiding meditation alone is not enough. It is only the basis for the practice of insight wisdom, which is the second stage. Without insight wisdom, it is not possible to destroy defilements from the root. Thus the main practice is actually insight wisdom, the wisdom of discernment. Using very sharp logical reasoning, you examine the nature of reality or the ultimate reality of all external and internal phenomena. Through this you see that the ultimate reality of all phenomena is away from the extremes of eternalism and nihilism, and devoid of all extreme views, such as existence, nonexistence, permanence, nothingness, and so forth. The attainment of such a state of understanding is the accomplishment of insight wisdom. Combining it with calm-abiding meditation allows you to dwell single-pointedly on the insight wisdom that has been realized.

Insight wisdom consists of three steps. The first is to establish all outer objects or outer appearances as your own mind. The second is to establish all mental objects as illusory. The third is to establish all illusions as devoid of inherent nature.

Outer appearances are your own mind.

The first step is to establish all outer appearances as your own mind. The meaning of this is that all the objects that you see and all the appearances or visions that you encounter every day—such as the elements, sentient beings, atoms, and so on—are not without a cause, are not created by an outside force, and are not inherently existing. In reality, they are all mentally projected. From beginningless time until now, our habits of perceiving these phenomena has left impressions, in the form of latent propensities, on our minds. As a result, when suitable conditions come together, these tendencies project the phenomena around us. In fact, there is no creator of these objects apart from our own minds.

This is similar to the phenomenon of dreams. In dreams we see many things, such as different countries, animals, and other beings. We have happy dreams, sad dreams, nightmares—dreams of all kinds. These dreams can cause joy, sadness, fear, and so on. Even so, there is no outside object. Dreams are nothing but our own minds. But while we are dreaming, our dreams appear as real as this present life.

Similarly, this life that we experience is also like a dream. There is no difference between dreams and this present life. Dreams are experienced by yourself; this life is also experienced by yourself. Dreams can provoke many types of feelings; this life can provoke many types of feelings. The only real difference is the length of time—dreams are much shorter than the present life. Apart from that, there is no difference.

In this way, all objects that appear externally are actually not separate from your own mind. If the outer world were separate from your mind, then its characteristics would always be the same for everyone, but we can see that this is not the case. For one person a certain place might seem to be a very happy place, but for another person it might be a very unhappy place. Furthermore, a single person may see it as very happy at one time and very unhappy at another time. In this way, it is easy to see that all the things you encounter are actually projections of your own mind.

Mental objects are illusory.

Having established that all outer appearances are your own mind, the second step is to establish all mental objects as illusory. As it is said in the sutras, "Just as the appearance of various illusory forms of horses, elephants, and carts made by magicians are not true whatsoever, just so should all *dharmas* (phenomena) be known." As this states, all these phenomena are like magical illusions. When a magician combines certain special ingredients with the power of an incantation, it is possible for us to see many things, such as elephants, horses, and so on, although none of these actually exist. In this way it is said that the various outer appearances are like a magical illusion.

When the causes are gathered together, something appears. But when we examine that thing to try to find out what it is, we cannot find it at all. Put another way, as long as a thing depends on causes and conditions, it is shown to be devoid of existing inherently. If it existed inherently, it would not depend on other causes and conditions. As soon as one of its causes is missing, it will not appear.

Television provides an example of this. An image appearing on a television screen depends upon many conditions, such as the presence of electricity, a functioning cable or antenna, the television signal, and so on. If any of these conditions are missing, even if the tiniest wire or circuit is broken or absent, the image will not appear. When all of the causes and conditions are gathered together, then the image appears. Even so, although the image appears, still it is not real.

Reflect on this, thinking that all mental appearances are like illusions in a magical show or like the moon's reflection in water. When the conditions gather together, the phenomena appear. Meditate until you have certain knowledge of this.

Illusions are devoid of inherent nature.

The third stage is to establish that all illusions are devoid of inherent nature. On the relative level, all these objects, which arise because of the gathering of causes and conditions, appear unceasingly. If we try to examine them, however, we cannot find anything that exists inherently. Put another way, on the relative level, because they are interdependently originated, visions or appearances never cease. On the absolute level, they are all emptiness. Emptiness does not mean that things do not exist; emptiness is just a word that we use to describe actual reality, which is beyond words such as existence, nonexistence, neither, or both. Reality is both unceasing clarity and emptiness, and the two do not contradict. As long as appearances and emptiness do not contradict, they become nondual appearance and emptiness, nondual sound and emptiness, and nondual awareness and emptiness. This is actual insight wisdom.

The union of calm abiding and insight wisdom

Having developed calm abiding and insight wisdom, the third stage is to merge these two together. This, too, is done step by step. The first step is to establish all outer appearances as mind, all mental objects as illusory, and illusory visions as devoid of inherent nature. Then the analytical mind that realizes this emptiness and that is beyond all description is merged with the actual or object reality, which has from the very beginning been free from all extremes. These two merge together inseparably, just like water mixing with water or melted butter mixing with melted butter. Meditate on this realization and remain in this state single-pointedly, like candlelight in the absence of wind. When there is no wind, a candle's light is very steady and tranquil and it glows very clearly. Meditate in this state.

With practice, you will gradually become more and more familiar with this state. The closer you are to ultimate truth, the more compassion arises for those sentient beings who do not realize this truth and as a result experience much suffering. Through the combination of compassion and the wisdom that realizes emptiness, all illusory visions are transformed into wisdom. Eventually, full enlightenment endowed with the three kayas and unceasing great activities will be accomplished.

This completes the explanation of the fourth line of *Parting from the Four Attachments*, "If grasping arises, you do not have the view."

CONCLUSION: THE DEDICATION OF MERIT

The third and final part of the teaching is the dedication of merit. At the end of every meditation session, it is important to dedicate the merit. Without dedication, the merit of whatever virtuous deeds have been accomplished can be destroyed by a strong opposing factor, such as anger or hatred. By dedicating the merit skillfully, however, not only is it unaffected by opposing factors, but it also increases continuously until we reach the ultimate goal.

To dedicate the merit, first think that all the merit you have gained through this very profound meditation is combined with the merit of all the virtuous deeds you have accumulated in the past, are accumulating now, and will accumulate in the future. Because all reality is mind, it is even possible to dedicate the merit that you have not yet accumulated. Then with all these combined together, think, "Through the power of performing these virtuous deeds, may I and all sentient beings attain enlightenment."

When dedicating the merit, recall that all phenomena are like a dream or like magical illusions. Aspire to dedicate your own merit just as the great bodhisattvas dedicated theirs, and in this way follow in their great footsteps.

This completes the teaching on *Parting from the Four Attachments*.

Instructions on
Parting from the Four Attachments

Jetsun Dragpa Gyaltsen (1147–1216)

Om svasti siddhi!

THE GREAT LAMA SAKYAPA, at the age of twelve, having practiced on Lord Manjushri for six months, one day clearly perceived Lord Manjushri red-gold and bathed in light on a precious throne, with the gesture of teaching, nobly seated with his two retinue bodhisattvas, one each on the right and the left. Manjushri spoke:

> If you have attachment to this life, you are not a religious person.
> If you have attachment to the world of existence, you do not have renunciation.
> If you have attachment to your own purpose, you do not have enlightenment mind.
> If grasping arises, you do not have the view.

Analyzing this, he realized that all essential practices of the path of perfection are integrated in the mind training of *Parting from the Four Attachments*, and he developed profound trust in the Dharma.

Shapathamithi!

Jetsun Dragpa Gyaltsen (1147–1216).
Collection of Shelley and Donald Rubin. Himalayan Art Resources 203.

I take refuge from my heart
in the kind lama and
the compassionate deities;
bestow your blessings upon me.

Nonreligious action is useless.
Practice according to the Dharma.
These instructions on *Parting from the Four Attachments*
I will expound for you to hear.

[The above sets forth the homage and intent to explain.]

If you have attachment to this life, you are not a religious person.
If you have attachment to the world of existence, you do not have
     renunciation.
If you have attachment to your own purpose, you do not have
     enlightenment mind.
If grasping arises, you do not have the view.

First, without attachment to this life,
practice morality, study, contemplation, and meditation.
Practicing with the aim of this life is not religious,
so put it aside.

First, to explain morality:
It is the root of accomplishing the higher realms,
a ladder to accomplish liberation,
and an antidote to remove suffering.

Morality is indispensable,
yet morality that has attachment to this life

is rooted in the eight worldly dharmas;
it draws accusations of immorality,

has jealousy toward the moral,
has hypocrisy concerning your own morality,
and is the seed to accomplishing the lower realms.
So put aside artificial morality.

Those who study and contemplate
have a wealth of accumulated knowledge,
have a lamp to dispel ignorance,
have knowledge to guide beings' paths,

and have the seed of the dharmakaya.
Study and contemplation are indispensable,
yet study and contemplation that are attached to this life
have a wealth of accumulated pride,

have contempt toward the unlearned,
have jealousy toward the learned,
have longing for wealth and followers,
and are the root to accomplishing the lower realms.

So put aside study and contemplation with the eight dharmas.
Any practitioner who meditates
has an antidote to remove defilements,
the root to accomplish the path of liberation,

and the seed to accomplish buddhahood.
Meditation is indispensable,
yet meditation that has attachment to this life
has crowds when in solitude,

has idle talk for recitation,
has criticism of the learned,
and has jealousy of other meditators and distraction
   in meditation.
So put aside meditation with the eight dharmas.

[The above is based on the *Treasury of Abhidharma*, wherein it is said, "Maintain morality, study, and contemplation, then thoroughly meditate." It directly explains the distinction between real and artificial, and it indirectly explains how to meditate on the difficulty of attaining precious human birth and the impermanence of life.]

To accomplish nirvana
requires abandoning attachment to the three worlds.
To abandon attachment to the three worlds
requires remembering the faults of samsara.

First, to explain the suffering of suffering,
it includes the suffering of the three lower realms.
If contemplated carefully, the hair stands on end,
for if it occurs, it is intolerable.

Not practicing Dharma, which ends this suffering,
they actively cultivate the lower realms.
How pitiful, wherever they are!

To explain the suffering of change,
higher beings are reborn lower,
Indra is reborn as an ordinary being,
the sun and moon become dark,

and a universal emperor is reborn as a servant.
Although this is asserted based on scripture,

ordinary beings cannot know it.
So observe human change for yourself:

The rich become poor;
the powerful become powerless;
many become one;
these and other changes are indescribable.

To explain all-pervasive suffering:
Work has no end;
suffering arises both alone and with many;
suffering occurs whether rich or poor.

We spend our lives preparing.
Every life ends amid preparations.
Preparations don't end even after death,
as the next life's preparation begins.

This heap of suffering:
How pitiful, to be attached to it!

[The above directly explains the faults of samsara. It indirectly explains what to collect and what to abandon in relation to cause and effect.]

Freedom from attachment brings nirvana,
and nirvana brings happiness.

Parting from the Four Attachments is a song of experience.
Self-liberation alone is without benefit.
The three worlds' beings are your parents.
To leave parents amid suffering—
how pitiful are seekers of self-liberation!

May the suffering of the three worlds ripen on me;
may all my virtues be taken by beings.
By the blessings of this virtue,
may all beings achieve buddhahood.

[The above indirectly explains the method of meditation on loving kindness
and compassion as the cause. It directly explains exchange of self and other as
the result.]

However you live,
there is no liberation with attachment to the nature of suchness.
To explain this in detail:

There is no liberation with attachment to existence.
There is no higher rebirth with attachment to nonexistence.
Attachment to both is not possible.
Joyfully rest in the state of nonduality.

[The above generally explains how to rest the mind in the state of nonduality
without attachment to either eternalism or nihilism.]

All phenomena are mental activities.
Search not for a creator of the four elements,
like Ishvara or others.
Joyfully rest in the state of mental suchness.

[The above explains the stages of the path according to the Mahayana Mind
Only school. The following explains the view of the uncommon Mahayana
Madhyamaka school.]

The nature of appearances is illusory
and arises through interdependence.

Their nature is indescribable.
Joyfully rest in the state of inexpressibility.

[The above indirectly explains how to do calm-abiding meditation; directly it explains how to do insight meditation and thus to establish all appearances as states of mind, the mind itself as illusory, insubstantial, interdependent, and inexpressible, and how to rest the mind in the state of nonduality, free from all extremes.]

By the merit of the virtue
of explaining *Parting from the Four Attachments*,
may all among the seven types of beings
be placed on the stage of buddhahood.

[The above explains the dedication and result.]

These instructions on *Parting from the Four Attachments* were written by the yogi Dragpa Gyaltsen at glorious Sakya Monastery.

Translated by Khenpo Kalsang Gyaltsen and Ani Kunga Chodron at Sakya Phuntsok Ling near Washington, DC, in 1998.

Pith Instructions on
Parting from the Four Attachments

SAKYA PANDITA KUNGA GYALTSEN (1182–1251)

Prostration to the feet of the holy lamas!

GENERALLY, those who have attained a body with the freedoms and endowments, met the Buddha's precious doctrine, and given rise to a genuine motivation should practice the unmistaken Dharma. For such people, it is important to practice parting from the four attachments. If you wonder, these practices are: nonattachment to this life, nonattachment to the three realms of samsara, nonattachment to self-purpose, and nonattachment to matter and its characteristics. To explain:

This life is like a water bubble. Since the time of death is uncertain, it is worthless to be attached to this life.

These three realms of samsara are like poisonous fruit: initially sweet but later harmful. Whoever is attached to them is deluded.

Attachment to your own purpose is like adopting an enemy's son: initially dear but later certainly harmful. Although attachment to your own purpose is initially pleasant, it will later cause descent into a lower birth.

Attachment to matter and its characteristics is like perceiving water in a mirage: it is initially seen as water, but it cannot be drunk. This

Sakya Pandita Kunga Gyaltsen (1182–1251).
Collection of Shelley and Donald Rubin. Himalayan Art Resources 42.

samsara may be perceived by deluded minds, yet when analyzed with wisdom, nothing can be shown to inherently exist.

Therefore, knowing that the mind should not engage in the past nor engage in the future, and that the consciousness should not even engage in the present, know that all phenomena are free of conceptual elaboration.

Thus, through nonattachment to this life, you will not be born in lower realms.

Through nonattachment to the three realms, you will not be born in samsara.

Through nonattachment to self-purpose, you will not be born an arhat or pratekyabuddha.

Through nonattachment to matter and its characteristics, you will swiftly reach perfect and full enlightenment.

These unmistaken instructions on *Parting from the Four Attachments*, the intent of the great glorious Sakyapa, were written by Sakya Pandita.

Translated by Khenpo Kalsang Gyaltsen and Ani Kunga at Tsechen Kunchab Ling in Walden, New York, during the month of Vesak, 2010. From the *Sakya Kabum*, volume *na*.

The Key to the Profound Meaning:
A Manual of Instructions on
Parting from the Four Attachments

GORAMPA SONAM SENGE (1429–89)

To you, whose great wisdom, like a divine path, pervades all know-
    able things;
whose compassion, like the moon, is the crowning ornament of sen-
    tient beings;
whose divine activity, like a wish-fulfilling gem, is a treasure for all
    needs and wishes;
O matchless protector, the lion of the Shakyas, grant good virtue to
    all beings.

You are Manjughosha, the confluence of the wisdom of all the con-
    querors of the three times;
you are Avalokiteshvara, who promised to protect all beings of the
    lower realms;
O great Sakyapa, who in this degenerate era took human form in
    order to lead beings,
your name alone is difficult to express; to you I respectfully bow.

IN REPLY to the pure-hearted one, who by the force of previously
accumulated merit has obtained the vessel of a human body with
which to accomplish the holy Dharma, and who spontaneously has

Gorampa Sonam Senge (1429–89).
Collection of the Rubin Museum of Art. Himalayan Art Resources 368.

gained prosperity and has performed activities for the Dharma and the upholders of the Dharma, I have here given this uncommon instruction on important aspects of the Mahayana.

With respect to this, the fully complete Buddha, who is endowed with a mind that acts for the benefit of all beings without being asked, taught the collection of Dharma just in accordance with the conditions, thoughts, and mental propensities of those to be tamed. All are collected together in the Paramitayana and the Vajrayana. In the former there are two: practicing the teachings that come from the principal scriptural explanations, and practicing the essential oral instructions.

If you practice by the authority of the main scriptural explanations, then it says in the protector Maitreya's *Ornament of Clear Realization*, "The meaning of the Perfection of Wisdom sutras is that the eight clear realizations are the stages of the path."

His *Ornament of the Sutras* states: "The intention of the various Mahayana sutras is to show that logical reasoning, faith in the Dharma, and so forth, are the stages of the path."

The supreme Arya Nagarjuna says in his *Jewel Garland*, "First of all, both higher birth and a certain level of happiness are to be accomplished; then the stages of the path are accomplished through the practices of faith and wisdom."

Acharya Aryadeva says:

> Having as an aim supreme enlightenment, which abandons the four erroneous views, the afflictions are destroyed along with their cause, which are a hindrance to the accomplishment of the bodhisattva's path. Becoming a vessel suitable for the ultimate truth, the main practice is then being shown the nectar of ultimate truth. These are the stages of the path.

Acharya Shantideva says:

> Based upon the perfectly endowed human form, you prac-
> tice the six perfections, which are the essence of the bodhi-
> sattva conduct, and you link this with perfectly pure prayer;
> these are the stages of the path leading to the attainment of
> buddhahood.

Venerable Lord Atisha said:

> The person of small scope abandons attachment to this life
> and attains benefit for just the next. The person of medium
> scope abandons the fruits of samsaric happiness and attains
> just liberation. The person of greater scope attains buddha-
> hood for the benefit of beings. These three kinds of persons
> are the stages of the path.

The glorious Chandrakirti said:

> In the case of an ordinary being practicing the three—
> compassion, enlightenment mind, and nondual mind—they
> will attain the state of an arya. Then by the ten perfections
> they will traverse the ten bodhisattva levels. These are the
> stages of the path that will accomplish the three bodies of
> the Buddha.

Although the excellent, good traditions by which the mighty ones
unerringly explain the Mahayana teachings are splendid, these scriptural traditions are for the highly intelligent to understand and not for
those of lesser intelligence.

Second is to practice the meaning of the oral instructions. In general, a great many have arisen, but chiefly there are two: that which Serlingpa gave to Venerable Lord Atisha, and that which the Protector Manjushri gave to Lama Sakyapa Kunga Nyingpo.

The first includes the difficulty of attaining the prerequisites, death and impermanence, the cause and effect of actions, and the faults of worldly existence. Through these four, you become a vessel that produces enlightenment mind. Having applied the preparatory practices of loving kindness and compassion for a long time, then perform the main practice, which is chiefly meditating on the enlightenment mind of exchanging self and others. Occasionally, also meditate upon ultimate enlightenment mind.

As to the branch practices of the path, they are: transforming unfavorable circumstances into the path to enlightenment, summarizing and demonstrating the practice of a lifetime, the gauge of mind training, the commitments of mind training, and instructions for mind training. This is an excellent path for practice. Although less visible, it is an extremely swift means of traveling the path.

In Tibet, Venerable Atisha gave this to the spiritual friend Dromtompa and one other. The spiritual friend also taught it to the three precious brothers and no one else. From them it spread widely. In the hermitages of Tibet, the Land of Snows, this path is as famous as the sun and moon. For this practice, look at other works, such as those of Gyalse Chodzong and his disciples and those of the great being Zhonu Gyalchog.

Now, as to the teaching that the protector Manjushri gave Lama Sakyapa, although this practice is similar in essence to the previous one, the depth of what needs to be explained and the levels of meaning are significantly higher than in the other. At the age of twelve, the great Lama Sakyapa Kunga Nyingpo practiced Manjushri, and after six months he directly saw the protector Manjushri, who said:

> If you have attachment to this life, you are not a religious
> person.
> If you have attachment to the world of existence, you do not
> have renunciation.
> If you have attachment to your own purpose, you do not have
> enlightenment mind.
> If grasping arises, you do not have the view.

These lines condense all of the practices of the Perfection Vehicle. Concerning the meaning: Having parted from attachment to this life, your mind proceeds toward the Dharma. Having parted from attachment to the world of existence, you traverse the path of Dharma. Having parted from attachment to your own purpose, the path is cleared of confusion. Having parted from attachment to the four extremes, illusory appearances arise as primordial wisdom.

1. HAVING PARTED FROM ATTACHMENT TO THIS LIFE, YOUR MIND PROCEEDS TOWARD THE DHARMA.

This first line contains the preparatory practice on the difficulty of obtaining the prerequisites, the main practice on death and impermanence, and the auxiliary practice on the cause and effect of actions.

First: Meditate on the difficulty of obtaining the prerequisites.

Seated upon a comfortable seat, take refuge in the guru and the Three Jewels many times and then pray that your mind may proceed in the Dharma, and so on. In order to produce enlightenment mind, think, "For the sake of all sentient beings I must attain buddhahood...."

Then think, "From the viewpoint of its nature, a precious human birth endowed with the eighteen prerequisites—the eight freedoms and ten endowments—is difficult to obtain. From the viewpoint of its cause, a precious human birth is difficult to obtain because it requires the accomplishment of mental virtue, and this virtue is very rare. From the viewpoint of its number, among the six types of sentient beings, there are more in each of the lower realms than in the realms above it. We can see this directly since the entire population of the earth cannot equal even the number of insects in a pond in the summertime or those living in a tree stump. Also, from the point of view of metaphors, a precious human birth is as difficult to obtain as it is for a lentil to adhere to a wall at which it has been thrown, or as difficult as it is for a sea tortoise to inadvertently stick its neck through a wooden yoke that is being blown around a great ocean. Therefore, though I have somehow now obtained this human body endowed with the prerequisites, I must meditate with the thought that it should not be wasted but rather used to achieve benefit for the next life.

Second: Meditate on death and impermanence.

As before, first take refuge and produce enlightenment mind. Then think in the following manner:

"There is no one living who, having been born, is able to remain living and not die; thus my death is certain. Furthermore, there is no assurance that I won't die this instant, since there are many causes of death and few causes of life; therefore, the timing of death is uncertain. When the time of death comes, nothing whatsoever, such as medicine or religious services, can avert it. Nothing whatsoever can stop death once it comes. Having contemplated that after death neither my friends nor my wealth, nor anything other than the Dharma, will follow me, I must part from attachment to this life."

Since this is the chief method of making the mind proceed toward the Dharma, even now when you are eating good food, wearing good clothes, and are surrounded by many friends, meditate on the thought,

"Now it is like this, but one day I will be separating from this, and I will have to go alone; so they are without essence and worthless." In this way, part from attachment to the activities of this life.

Third: Meditate on the cause and effect of actions.

Having taken refuge and produced enlightenment mind as before, think: "I have obtained this precious human birth with the prerequisites that are so difficult to obtain, but this is impermanent. Before dying I must abandon all nonvirtue and accomplish as much virtue as possible."

The reason for this is that the fully ripened effect of committing the ten nonvirtuous deeds is rebirth in the three lower realms. Regarding the effect that is consistent with the cause, it is explained that through killing you will have a short life; through taking what is not given, you will be without wealth; and so on. The instrumental cause of becoming familiarized or accustomed to a nonvirtuous deed is the wish to repeat that action again and again, and since the result of these nonvirtuous actions is rebirth in the lower realms and the like, there will be no chance for liberation. Through the environmental effect, you will take birth in a foul-smelling and dusty land. Contemplating this arouses the desire to certainly abandon nonvirtuous deeds.

Likewise, the fully ripened effect of the ten virtuous deeds is birth in a happy realm. The effect that is consistent with the cause is that by abandoning killing, you will have a long life, and so on. The instrumental result of virtuous conduct is the wish to commit that virtuous action again and again. The environmental effect is birth in a pleasant-smelling land, and so on. Since this is so, think, "I must certainly accomplish this. Now having understood the meaning of karma, cause and result, and understood what is to be accepted and rejected, it is vital that I put this into practice."

2. HAVING PARTED FROM CLINGING TO THE WORLD OF EXISTENCE, YOU TRAVERSE THE PATH OF DHARMA.

For this, think about the faults of the three realms of existence. Having taken refuge and produced enlightenment mind as before, think, "The three realms of existence do not pass beyond the nature of suffering. In the hot hells, there is the suffering of the body being burned with fire, cut with weapons, and so on. In the cold hells, there is the suffering of extreme cold splitting the flesh and bones into several parts, and so on. In the neighboring hells, there is the suffering of being in a place with glowing hot coals, and so on. If that type of suffering were to come to my present body, I would not be able to bear even a tiny fraction of it.

"The hungry ghosts experience the suffering of hunger, thirst, heat, cold, hardships, and fear. In the realm of animals, there is the devouring of one another; for animals that are scattered about, there is the suffering of being used and being slaughtered."

"Also, for humans, the high become low and there is the inability to obtain even a little of what is desired, the meeting with what is not wanted, and the separation from relatives. These and others are the sufferings we can directly perceive right now.

"For the gods of the desire realm, when the signs of death and its approach occur, their mental suffering is even greater than the physical suffering of beings in hell. Although the gods of the form realm and formless realms do not directly experience suffering now, one day they will fall and will have to experience all the sufferings of the lower realms.

"Therefore, these three realms of existence do not pass beyond the nature of suffering. Thus I must abandon the world of existence and must attain the stage of liberation."

If the above section is compared with the stages of the path of the three types of persons, then the path of the person of small and medium scope is completed. Following Serlingpa's path, this then completes the four Dharmas of the preliminary foundation.

3. HAVING PARTED FROM CLINGING TO YOUR OWN PURPOSE, THE PATH IS CLEARED OF CONFUSION.

For this, meditate on the three: loving kindness, compassion, and enlightenment mind.

As to the first, it is not proper to gain liberation from the suffering of existence for yourself alone. Think, "All beings of the three realms have acted as my very kind parents on many occasions." Reflect in particular, "My mother of this life first bore me in her womb. After birth I was like an emaciated worm, but she kept me alive and kindly protected me with food, clothes, and so on. Recalling the magnitude of my mother's kindness, and seeing that my mother has been so kind, I must place her in a state of happiness."

Then be mindful that your other relatives, the enemies who do you harm, and even the suffering beings in the three realms and the like have also shown you kindness by being your mother again and again throughout beginningless samsara. Meditate to produce loving kindness in your mind, which is the desire to place them in a state of happiness.

As to the second, meditate on compassion. Recall whatever kindness your present mother has shown, and the need for this kind mother to also be freed from suffering. As now she is entangled with suffering, have compassion for her. Then think, "Wouldn't it be proper if she were freed from suffering!" In the same way, recall that all beings have previously given you similar kindness. Thus meditate on compassion, which desires that all be free from suffering.

If you do not produce these two in your mind—loving kindness and compassion—then enlightenment mind will not truly arise. Since these two are the root of all Mahayana teachings, it is very important to exert yourself in practicing them.

As to the third, meditation on enlightenment mind, this includes: wishing enlightenment mind, the enlightenment mind that equates self and others, and the enlightenment mind that exchanges self and others.

For the first of these three, think, "Although I wish that my kind parents of the three realms of existence would be endowed with happiness and freed from suffering, right now I do not have the ability to bring this about. Not only this, but the great ones of the universe—Brahma, Indra, and so on—and the shravakas and pratyekabuddhas, who have gone beyond this universe, do not have this ability. Since it is only the fully and perfectly enlightened buddhas who have this ability, then, for the sake of all sentient beings, I must attain the state of full enlightenment. I must liberate all my kind parents from the ocean of existence." There is no other cause for the attainment of buddhahood. If this enlightenment mind is produced in your mental continuum, then the virtuous root of whatever practice you perform becomes a cause for attaining full enlightenment. Therefore, this has been praised many times in Mahayana sutras.

Next is the meditation on equating self and others. Think, "Just as I want happiness, so do all sentient beings want happiness. Therefore, just as I would try to accomplish my own happiness, so I must also try to accomplish the happiness of all sentient beings. Just as I do not want suffering, all sentient beings also do not want suffering. Therefore, just as I would remove my own suffering, so I must remove the suffering of all sentient beings."

Finally, there is the meditation of exchanging self for others. Visualizing your present mother in front of yourself, think, "Although this mother has been so kind, she is dwelling in suffering. I feel compassion for her. May all my mother's sufferings and her nonvirtues ripen upon me so that I experience them! May all of my happiness and virtue ripen upon my mother so that she attains buddhahood." Similarly, meditate upon each of your other relatives, those sentient beings you have not met or heard of, your enemies who have done you harm, suffering beings in the lower realms, and so forth.

Finally meditate upon gathering the heap of sufferings of all sentient beings upon yourself and giving your own happiness and virtue to all sentient beings. This becomes the cause for their attainment of whatever present prosperity they wish for and ultimately for their attainment of buddhahood.

Since this is the heart of the Mahayana practice, and the secret teaching of all the buddhas of the three times, there are many other explanations of the reason we meditate in this manner, the precepts of the instructions, and the meditation method for cutting through doubts. Thus, I will not elaborate on them here.

This wishing enlightenment mind must certainly be preceded by taking refuge and producing enlightenment mind as previously shown. Besides that, also meditate well upon guru devotion. Then, at the conclusion of every meditation session, seal it with dedications and other prayers. At all times, in all activities of walking, sleeping, and sitting, remain mindful.

4. If freed from attachment to the four extremes, illusory appearances arise as primordial wisdom.

In the pith instructions of other traditions, both calm abiding and insight wisdom are given; and within insight wisdom is the meditation on personal selflessness, the meditation on phenomenal selflessness, and so on. However, in this tradition, there are three meditations: establishing outer appearances as the mind, establishing mind as illusion, and establishing illusions as devoid of inherent nature. During post-meditation periods, remain in the practice of seeing phenomena as a dream or viewing them as an illusion. If you meditate by yourself, without relying on the guru's pith instructions, then the basic confusion will become greater. Furthermore, understanding illusory appearances as primordial wisdom cannot be understood from the written word alone. Therefore, it is not elaborated here.

Nevertheless, for immediate benefit, it is important that, whatever root of virtue you accomplish, you do not see yourself as a virtuous actor doing virtuous things, or think "I myself have done this or that virtue," or show conceit. However, for the purpose of exhorting others to virtue, it is without fault to state, without pride, "I have myself performed this virtue." That being so, straight away at the time of accomplishing the root of virtue and performing worldly tasks, remember to think, "It is an illusion. It is a dream." It is very important to put effort into remembering this, as it will become a cause of understanding the view.

In regard to this path, there are four stages, of which the first is, "By accomplishing the purpose of future lives, your mind turns toward the Dharma." The second is, "Accomplishing the path of liberation by abandoning cyclic existence, you travel the Dharma path." The third is, "Applying yourself to the Mahayana by abandoning the wish for the Hinayana, confusions on the path are dispelled." The fourth and final is, "Applying yourself to actual ultimate reality by entirely abandoning grasping at mental activities, confusion transforms into primordial wisdom."

Regard these as the fundamentals of the path to take into experience. Then right now: In order to make meaningful use of your body, prostrate and circumambulate. In order to make meaningful use of your voice, praise the buddhas and bodhisattvas and read aloud from the profound sutras. In order to make meaningful use of your mind, meditate on loving kindness, compassion, and enlightenment mind.

And in order to make meaningful use of your resources, make offerings to the Three Jewels and offer respect, homage, and so on to the Sangha. If you join this with pure aspiration prayers, it is certain that you will obtain complete buddhahood, which is without defects and possesses all good qualities.

Now to outline in verse the key points contained herein:

> A body to support practice of the holy Dharma is difficult to
>   obtain,
> and its nature is impermanent and swift to disintegrate.
> From thorough understanding of adopting virtue and
>   abandoning sin,
> with sincere conscientiousness, take very great care.
> That is the first stage.

> Within the ocean of samsara are sentient beings without limit.
> Seeing them swallowed by the sea monster of suffering,
> generate the renunciation that seeks
> the dry ground of the liberation of nirvana.
> This is the second stage.

> As extensive as space, wandering sentient beings
> have again and again been my parents.
> By remembering the kindness and benefit they gave,
> with loving kindness, compassion, and the excellent
>   enlightenment mind,
> accomplish the purposes of others.
> This is the third stage.

> Everything that is experienced is mind;
> that very mind, a mere collection of causes and conditions,
>   is an illusion.

Knowing illusion to be free of all elaboration,
meditate on ultimate truth.
This is the fourth stage.

On all occasions, make offerings to the Three Jewels;
gradually abandon nonvirtuous things;
care for the protectorless and the impoverished through
  generosity.
Then if you dedicate, perfectly purified from the three aspects,
your temporary and ultimate purposes will certainly be
  accomplished.

I have compiled this, the essence of the Mahayana path, with the thought of benefiting your practice. I offer it to you, patron of the Dharma. Through its practice, may all of your purposes be attained.

The bodhisattva in the form of a holy layman, Ralo Dorje, the patron of Dharma practitioners, unwaveringly faithful to the precious Dharma, requested religious advice concerning the holy Dharma, saying that beneficial advice in a precise form was needed. This was composed at a sacred hermitage of Dokhar on the third day of the rising of the constellation Pleiades by the Buddhist monk Sonam Senge. May auspicious omens and blessings arise!

Adapted from a translation by Geshe Sherab Gyaltsen Amipa based on a translation by Ngawang Samten Chophel originally published in a booklet for free distribution titled: *A Collection of Instructions on Parting from the Four Attachments.* Singapore Buddha Sasana Society (Sakya Tenphel Ling), 1982.

Heart Nectar: A Song of Experience on
Parting from the Four Attachments

JAMYANG KHYENTSE WANGPO (1820–92)

By the blessings of Lord Guru Manjushri,
may all beings equal to space practice the holy Dharma,
take the Dharma as their path,
allay all delusions, and dissolve all illusions into the dharmadhatu.

Even having obtained the freedoms and endowments as a
   foundation,
if you have attachment to this life, you are not a religious person.
So endeavor to adopt virtues and discard nonvirtues,
because time passes without even a moment's pause.

Even having turned your mind toward the holy Dharma,
if you have attachment to the three realms, you have no
   renunciation.
So develop the unadulterated thought of liberation,
because the very nature of samsara is suffering.

Even cherishing the peace and joy of liberation,
if you have attachment to your own purpose, you have no
   enlightenment mind.

Jamyang Khyentse Wangpo (1820–92).
Image courtesy of Alex Gardner. Himalayan Art Resources 57082.

So train in kindness, compassion, and enlightenment mind,
because all sentient beings are your very kind parents.

Even having trained in relative enlightenment,
if grasping arises, you do not have the view.
So strive for the realm of reality free from activity,
because you need to uproot the view of self.

These essential words were taught by Manjushri to the greatly kind
Sakyapa. By the merit of this song, may all mother sentient beings
swiftly reach enlightenment.

Translated into English by Khenpo Kalsang Gyaltsen and Reverend Jamyang
Tharchin at Sakya Phuntsok Ling, Washington, DC, 2008.

The Lineage of
Parting from the Four Attachments

Buddha

Manjushri

Sachen Kunga Nyingpo (1092–1158)

Sonam Tsemo (1142–82)

Dragpa Gyaltsen (1147–1216)

Sakya Pandita (1182–1251)

Chogyal Phagpa (1235–80)

Zhang Konchog Pal (1240–1308)

Choje Dragphugpa Sonam Pal (1277–1350)

Dampa Sonam Gyaltsen (1312–75)

Palden Tsultrim (1333–99)

Sharchen Yeshe Gyaltsen (d. 1406)

Ngorchen Kunga Zangpo (1382–1456)

Konchog Gyaltsen Pal (1388–1469)

Gorampa Sonam Senge (1429–89)

Sangye Rinchen (1450–1524)

Namkha Wangchug (b. fifteenth century)

Kunga Legdrub (b. fifteenth century)

Jampa Kunga Chodrag (b. sixteenth century)

Kunga Nampar Gyal (b. sixteenth century)

Khyenrab Tenzin Zangpo (b. sixteenth century)

Jampa Ngawang Lhundrub (1633–1703)

Morchen Kunga Lhundrub (1654–1726)

Nesarwa Kunga Legpai Jungne (1704–60)

Kunga Lodro (1729–83)

Chime Tenpai Nyima (b. eighteenth century)

Dorje Rinchen (1819–67)

Jamyang Khyentse Wangpo (1820–92)

Loter Wangpo (1847–1914)

Ngawang Lodro Zhenphen Nyingpo (1876–1953)

Dedication Prayer

The following prayer has been recited by great masters of the Sakya lineage for centuries.

By the merit of this, may we
attain the state of omniscience and defeat evil enemies;
from the samsaric ocean waves of birth, illness, aging, and death,
may all sentient beings be liberated.

Through this dedication, praised as supreme
by the victorious buddhas of the past, present, and future,
I dedicate all of these roots of virtue
to accomplishing the deeds of Samantabhadra.

May the Sakya teachings, which illuminate the Dharma,
and which are an excellent protector guarding the northern regions,
increase in this land of glacial peaks,
which is filled with an ocean of learned and realized masters.

May the spiritual and secular influence of splendid Sakya,
the vajra seat in the center of glacial Tibet, increase.
May the hereditary lineage of emanations continue without break,
and may all its activities equal the expanse of space.

Glossary

Abhidharma. The Buddha's higher trainings on philosophical topics.

Achala. "Immovable One"; a deity bestowing wisdom and protection.

arya. One who has attained the path of seeing or above.

Avalokiteshvara. The bodhisattva of great compassion.

brahman. A member of the Hindu priestly caste.

Brahma's realm. The form and formless realms, the pinnacle of life in cyclic existence.

buddha. A fully enlightened one, with every form of obscuration removed and every possible good quality accomplished.

bhumi. One of the stages of a bodhisattva's realization leading up to buddhahood. The bhumis, normally enumerated as ten, begin at the path of seeing and culminate in full enlightenment.

Chakrasamvara. A tantric tutelary deity who is the essence of wisdom.

creation and completion. The two stages of tantric practice.

dakini. Female tantric helper deity.

defilement (*klesha*). Stains of the mind experienced as emotional disturbances. The root defilement is ignorance, which conditions desire and hatred, and these three in turn drive all the others. Along with contaminated karma, defilements keep us locked in samsara.

desire realm. The realm in which most sentient beings cycle through rebirths. It includes the three lower realms of hell beings, hungry ghosts, and animals and the three higher realms of humans, demi-gods, and some of the gods.

Dharma. The Buddha's teachings and realizations. Lowercase *dharmas* means "phenomena."

dharmadhatu. "Sphere of reality"; the essence of phenomena, which is emptiness.

dharmakaya. "Body of reality"; one of the three bodies, or aspects, of a perfectly enlightened buddha. Can just refer to ultimate truth, a buddha's realization.

eight freedoms. Eight of the eighteen prerequisites of perfect human birth. The first four are freedom from the nonhuman states of birth as a hell being, a hungry ghost, an animal, or a long-lived god. Four are within the human realm, namely, freedom from birth among barbarians, birth among people with wrong beliefs, birth in a place where a buddha has not appeared, and birth as a person whose physical or mental impairment prevents their receiving the Dharma.

eight worldly dharmas. These eight are worldly mindstates given in four pairs: concerns for gain and loss, pleasure and pain, fame and disrepute, praise and blame.

eighteen prerequisites. Prerequisites necessary for a life in which it is possible to practice the Dharma. Such a life is known as a *precious human birth*. The prerequisites include freedom from eight unfavorable conditions and endowment with ten favorable conditions. *See also* eight freedoms; ten endowments

enlightenment mind (*bodhichitta*). The resolve to attain enlightenment for the benefit of all sentient beings. Enlightenment mind may be divided into *wishing enlightenment mind* and *engaging enlightenment mind* to refer to the phases of its development from aspiration to actual practice. Or it may be divided into *relative enlightenment mind* and *ultimate enlightenment mind* to refer, respectively, to the altruisic wish and to the realization of primordial wisdom free of elaboration.

four erroneous views. Perceiving oneself to be pure, happy, permanent, and possessed of a self.

genuine primordial wisdom. The basic nature of every sentient being's mind, which is empty of inherent nature and free of conceptual thought.

Great Compassionate One (*Mahakarunika*). A form of Avalokiteshvara.

Hevajra. A tutelary deity who is the integration of compassion and wisdom.

Hinayana. A school of Buddhism that focuses primarily on the four noble truths and takes arhatship as the highest goal rather than buddhahood.

interdependent origination. The theory that all phenomena arise due to causes and conditions rather than existing inherently.

Ishvara. An Indian creator god.

kaya. "Body" or aspect, especially of a buddha. The *three kayas*, or three bodies of a buddha, are the dharmakaya, the sambhogakaya, and the nirmanakaya.

krishnasara. A type of deer with a very gentle heart.

kusha grass. A stiff grass often used for brooms that is used ritually to symbolize cleansing.

Lamdre. Literally, "path and result"; the special instructions on Hevajra tantra unique to the Sakya tradition.

lingam. A stylized phallus worshiped by Hindus as a symbol of the god Shiva.

Madhyamaka. The Middle Way. A philosophical subschool of Mahayana Buddhism that holds that the nature of all phenomena is characterized by neither the extreme of existence nor the extreme of nonexistence.

Mahakala. "Great Black One"; a Dharma protector.

mahamudra. Literally "great seal"; realization of the ultimate nature of one's mind, its lack of inherent nature.

mahaparinirvana. The end of an enlightened being's physical life.

mahasiddha. A greatly accomplished meditator, often referring in particular to the early Indian masters in the tantric lineages.

Mahayana. "Great Vehicle"; one of the two major schools of Buddhism, the Mahayana emphasizes following the conduct and view of bodhisattvas, who strive for enlightenment to save all beings.

mala. A rosary usually made of 108 or 111 beads used for counting mantra recitations.

Manjughosha. Manjushri.

Manjushri. The bodhisattva of wisdom.

Middle Way. *See* Madhyamaka

Mind Only. A philosophical subschool of Mahayana Buddhism that holds that all phenomena are one's own mind.

Nalanda. A great Buddhist seat of learning in ancient India and the source of Tibetan Buddhism's dominant philosophical traditions.

nirmanakaya. "Body of emanations"; one of the three bodies of a perfectly enlightened buddha. Typically refers to the human form emanated by a buddha in order to benefit beings.

nirvana. Personal liberation; the cessation of suffering and its causes.

path of seeing. The third of the five paths, or progressive levels of realization, leading to buddhahood. On this path, a practitioner realizes ultimate truth directly for the first time, and a Mahayana practitioner enters the first bodhisattva bhumi.

Paramitayana. The "Perfection Vehicle"; the nontantric practice of the gradual path of pursuing enlightenment primarily through the practices of refuge, enlightenment mind, and the six perfections.

Prajnaparamita. The Perfection of Wisdom scriptures, which teach the view of emptiness.

pratyekabuddha. "Solitary realizer"; a Hinayana practioner who attains nirvana for himself alone without relying on a teacher in the life that he became a pratyekabuddha.

sambhogakaya. "Body of enjoyment"; one of the three bodies of a perfectly enlightened buddha. Refers to a buddha's exalted form visible in the pure buddhafields and to highly realized beings.

samsara. The cycle of suffering and rebirth fueled by defilements and karma.

Sangha. The community of followers of the Buddha, especially bodhisattvas who have reached the irreversible stage of the path.

Serlingpa. A tenth-century teacher of Atisha who lived in Suvarnadvipa, now known as Indonesia. He taught Atisha practices for developing enlightenment mind.

shamatha. Concentration meditation, also known as calm-abiding meditation.

Shiva. A Hindu deity.

shravaka. "Hearer" or "disciple"; A Hinayana practioner who attains personal liberation or nirvana by relying on a teacher.

six perfections. The Mahayana practices prescribed for a bodhisattva: the perfections of generosity, moral conduct, patience, diligence, meditation, and wisdom.

skillful means (*upaya*). Practice of the four means of gathering adherents and the six perfections.

stage of patience. This is the third of four stages of the path of preparation, which occurs just before the direct perception of ultimate truth on the path of seeing.

svabhavakaya. The indivisible aspect of the three holy bodies of a buddha.

tantra. The quick path to buddhahood through meditating on a deity, reciting mantras, and adopting the pure vision of oneself as already enlightened.

ten bodhisattva levels. *See* bhumi

ten endowments. The ten endowments necessary for a life in which one can practice Dharma, five acquired by oneself and five acquired from others. The five acquired by oneself are birth: as a human, in a central realm, with sound sense organs, without having committed heinous crimes, and with sincere faith in the Buddha's teachings. The five acquired from others are birth at a time during which: a buddha has come into this world, a buddha has bestowed the teachings, the teachings continue to be upheld as a living tradition, the followers are practicing, and sponsors are supporting the Dharma.

three bodies of a buddha. *See* kaya

vajra. A Sanskrit term meaning "indestructible." It refers to the ultimate wisdom of emptiness. Also, a ritual implement held in tantric practice and commonly depicted in Buddhist iconography.

Vajra Nairatmya. Hevajra's consort, whose name means "without self."

Vajra Verses. The root text of the Lamdre tradition composed by Virupa.

Vajrapani. A bodhisattva who manifests spiritual power. He wields a vajra in his right hand.

Vajrayana. The tantric path.

Vikramashila. A large Buddhist university in ancient India that produced many great scholars.

Vinaya. The portion of the Buddhist scriptures that deals with morality and discipline.

vipashyana. Insight wisdom, or the meditation to develop the realization of ultimate truth.

vira. Male tantric helper deity.

yogi. An ascetic practitioner of meditation.

About the Author

HIS HOLINESS SAKYA TRIZIN is the revered forty-first throne holder of the Sakya school of Tibetan Buddhism, which dates back to 1073. He is a member of the Khon family, who have been important teachers of Buddhism in Tibet since the eighth century. A brilliant master, he manifests profound wisdom and compassion, and his command of English renders his teachings particularly beneficial to students in the West.

He was born in 1945 in Sakya, Tibet, and in 1959 escaped with tens of thousands of Tibetan people to India, where he continues to live and work tirelessly to rebuild the Sakya tradition. He has guided the establishment of over thirty monasteries in India and Nepal and has helped found Sakya centers around the world. His seat in North America is Tsechen Kunchab Ling in Walden, New York. *Freeing the Heart and Mind* is his first book to be made widely available.

About Wisdom Publications

WISDOM PUBLICATIONS is dedicated to making available authentic Buddhist works for the benefit of all. We publish translations of Buddhist sacred texts, commentaries and teachings of past and contemporary Buddhist masters, and original works by the world's leading Buddhist scholars. We publish our titles with the appreciation of Buddhism as a living philosophy and with the special commitment to preserve and transmit important works from all the major Buddhist traditions.

Wisdom Publications
199 Elm Street
Somerville, Massachusetts 02144 USA
Telephone: 617-776-7416
Fax: 617-776-7841
Email: info@wisdompubs.org
www.wisdompubs.org

Wisdom is a nonprofit, charitable 501(c)(3) organization affiliated with the Foundation for the Preservation of the Mahayana Tradition (FPMT).